THE WIT & WISDOM OF

TEST MATCH SPECIAL

COMPILED BY
DAN WADDELL

BBC
BOOKS

BBC Books, an imprint of Ebury Publishing
20 Vauxhall Bridge Road,
London SW1V 2SA

BBC Books is part of the Penguin Random House group of companies
whose addresses can be found at global.penguinrandomhouse.com

This book is published to accompany the radio series entitled
Test Match Special broadcast on BBC Radio 4 and 5 Live Sports Extra.

Head of BBC Radio Sport: Richard Burgess
Commissioning Editor: Richard Maddock
BBC Cricket Producer: Adam Mountford

First published by BBC Books in 2015

www.eburypublishing.co.uk

A CIP catalogue record for this book is available from the British Library

ISBN 9781849908719

Commissioning Editor: Albert DePetrillo
Project Editor: Kate Fox
Design: Seagull Design
Illustration: Pete Ellis www.drawgood.com

Penguin Random House is committed to a sustainable future for
our business, our readers and our planet. This book is made from
Forest Stewardship Council® certified paper.

Printed and bound in Great Britain by Clays Ltd, St Ives plc

CONTENTS

FOREWORD
BY JONATHAN AGNEW

Life is full of crossroads. We have all encountered them along the way. Do I turn left or right? Take a chance with that job or stay where I am? Marry this person, or not? And those decisions are not merely restricted to the human race. Even the longest-running radio sports programme in the world has to confront challenges in order to survive in a rapidly changing environment.

The greatest threat to *Test Match Special* reared its head in 1992 when its faithful Radio 3 Medium Wave frequency, 1215 MW, was sold under government legislation to Virgin Radio. For one summer, *Test Match Special* shared Radio 3's FM frequency but it was not a happy relationship not least because of the impending launch of Classic FM. Despite sounding wonderful in glorious stereo for the first and only time in its long history, *TMS* could not continue on Radio 3 and the following summer, the Ashes of 1993, we sat very uncomfortably on the fledgling Radio 5 along with musical jingles, breaks for news on weekdays and competition from other sports on weekends. It was not quite the case of reading out racing results between overs, but as we worked that summer we quickly realized that this signalled the likely future for *Test Match Special* and, therefore, its immediate demise. It would have been the end long before Geoff Boycott ever appeared on the programme.

A crossroads had been reached and a choice had to be made. Continue straight ahead for Radio 5, turn right for the maverick but well-intended option of a private radio station funded by Sir Paul Getty, the oil billionaire and close friend of Brian Johnston, or finally recognize that a thoughtful speech programme renowned for its wit and wisdom belonged all the time on Radio 4, which had the option of splitting its emergency Long Wave frequency from its regular programming and offer us a new home. Politically, it was not a straightforward decision and some compromises had to be agreed. But *Test Match Special* made that crucial left turn that not only guaranteed its day-to-day survival, but being under the Radio 4 umbrella it ensured that we were a model Radio 4 programme: containing speech, gentle humour, intelligence and that unhurried feeling that is such a key element to cricket commentary.

The decision by the England and Wales Cricket Board to take cricket off BBC television screens in 1999, and then from terrestrial television altogether in 2006, might still have damaging consequences for the game but it has been to *Test Match Special*'s benefit in terms of the burgeoning audience and, because of the reach of the programme, its role in the game. More people listen to *TMS* now than ever before, including on digital radio via 5 Live Sports Extra. The internet allows us to broadcast all over the world (when cricket's authorities permit) but while Johnners might not recognize some of what we do now and how we do it, the abiding principles of a very individual radio programme that touches millions of people remain.

The secret is communication; the unique ability of radio to reach out and touch someone in a way that television never can. There is something very intimate about listening to cricket commentary through earphones in the depths of a winter's night. We transport you to distant places across the globe where the sun is always shining and England are playing cricket. Of course everything is marvellous; we must never disappoint or shatter the illusion that everything is never anything but wonderful. It is a small price to pay for the privilege of enjoying such a close relationship with our listeners.

They are a loyal bunch, the *TMS* faithful, who know as well as anyone what makes the programme tick, who they like to listen to and who they do not and why. Diversity, therefore, is very important when it comes to picking the *Test Match Special* team for every match. We need a combination of voices, backgrounds and character, all of which provide a balance to the programme and give something to everyone. The same procedure is applied to our many and varied guests, who have become such an important part of *TMS*. In those dim and distant days before Radio 4 LW, the only interval that required to be filled was Saturday's 'View from the Boundary'. Otherwise, every lunch and tea break, we would hand back to the studio and leave it to them. Those slots have become my favourite aspect of the programme. The commentary is the nuts and bolts, of course, but nowhere else on the BBC is there the opportunity to conduct interviews with the Prime Minister, with Lily Allen, Elton John, Colin Montgomerie or Alice Cooper (Geoff Boycott famously said: 'Nice to meet you, Alice' to Mrs

Cooper) that last for a full, uninterrupted half-hour with nowhere else to go. Those chats help lend *TMS* the genuine feeling of friendship, goodwill and the love of cricket that unites us all.

Carrying the *TMS* baton is something I never take lightly. The history and the traditions of this unique programme are too special for that. And, like the cricketers whose successes and failures we are describing through our open commentary box window, we are responsible for ensuring that future generations can experience the broadcasting phenomenon that is *Test Match Special*.

Jonathan Agnew, 2015

THE ART OF BATTING

HOWARD MARSHALL: The total – Hutton's total, 332. It sounds like the total of the whole side. The England total 707 for 5, and the gasometer sinking lower and lower. Here's Fleetwood-Smith again to Hutton. Hutton hits him. Oh, beautiful stroke! There's the record …

England v Australia, The Oval, August 1937

• • •

JOHN ARLOTT: He [Denis Compton] played so late that his stroke was within a sparrow's blink of being posthumous.

England v Australia, 1948

• • •

JOHN ARLOTT: Bedser heaves his shoulders, swings his arms back behind him until they meet, rolls his sleeve again, and comes pounding in ever-optimistically from the Radcliffe Road End, bowls to Weekes … and Weekes throws his bat at a ball wide outside his off stump – a most impudent stroke. That ball was a yard wide of the off stump – almost any other batsman in the world would have let it go by, but not Weekes.

England v West Indies, Trent Bridge, July 1950

• • •

In the course of a huge partnership, Colin Cowdrey and Peter May had broken the spell that spinner Sonny Ramadhin had held over the England team.

REX ALSTON: And England must be looking for runs now. Smith bowls short, Cowdrey has placed it gently towards third man, and the extra applause is because the partnership is now worth a monumental figure of 400. I think the imagination starts to boggle at all this business about records. We're getting tired of it – I should think [scorer] Roy Webber is drooling records, somewhere else along in this box …

England v West Indies, Edgbaston, June 1957

• • •

JOHN ARLOTT: It's Hall to bowl now to Dexter. He comes in from the Nursery End at full spit and bowls, and Dexter plays that very calmly back down the pitch off the middle of the bat as if Hall were a medium-pacer. There is about Dexter, when he chooses to stand up to fast bowling with determination, a sort of air of command that lifts him or seems to lift him above ordinary players … He seems to find time to play the fastest of bowling and still retain dignity, something near majesty as he does it.

England v West Indies, Lord's, June 1963

• • •

JOHN ARLOTT: And O'Neil goes out and disapprovingly prods the spot, rather like an old lady with an umbrella.

England v Australia, 1961

• • •

JOHN ARLOTT: … there it is! Four runs right of cover's left hand. It crosses the rope, beats Lawry. Boycott 102. Arthur Wrigley passes me a note to say a hundred in 3 hours and 55 minutes with 9 fours, and I believe by no means the last Test hundred we'll see from this man.

England v Australia, The Oval, August 1964

• • •

His bat has as many holes in it as a Henry Moore sculpture.

JOHN ARLOTT

• • •

Tom Graveney had returned to the England team after a three-year absence.

JOHN ARLOTT: Let us say that in a day when many people think the rest of the England batting failed there was this man, the senior of them all, demonstrating that it wasn't quite so difficult as some people might make it look. It becomes tragic now that he's been out of Test cricket for so long. It's said, 'All right he's 39, he can't last long,' but Jack Hobbs made over a hundred centuries after he was 40 and this man has something of the same ease as Jack Hobbs. Something of the rightness about when to go forward and when to go back …

England v West Indies, Lord's, June 1966

• • •

JOHN ARLOTT: Kanhai pushes that halfway up the wicket, wants a quick single. Sobers sends him back and makes little soothing motions with his hand to Kanhai as if to say, 'There, there, we've got all week.' He's not a man, in general, over-afflicted with patience when it comes to batting.

England v West Indies, 1966

• • •

John Arlott was in the box as the West Indies, led by Clive Lloyd, put Australia to the sword and gave what is considered to be one of his finest passages of commentary …

JOHN ARLOTT: They've scored off the last 15 balls. Now difficult, not only to bowl a maiden over, but apparently to bowl a maiden ball …

JOHN ARLOTT: And Lloyd hits him high over midwicket for four. The stroke of a man knocking a thistle top off with a walking stick. No trouble at all …

JOHN ARLOTT: And umpire Bird having a wonderful time, signalling everything in the world, including stop to traffic coming on from behind.

JOHN ARLOTT (*on a rare dot ball*): That is the first time in hours that the ball has passed through unviolated.

West Indies v Australia, World Cup final, Lord's, June 1975

• • •

This match marked Graham Gooch's England debut ...

DON MOSEY: ... [Gooch] a very burly broad-shouldered young man, 21, shock of dark hair, Walker in, bowls, Gooch looks for a run on the leg side and he's out! Caught on the leg side, trying to glance, he's caught by Marsh and he joins the distinguished ranks of the great cricketers who have got a duck on their first Test appearance.

England v Australia, Edgbaston, July 1975

• • •

Northamptonshire's David Steele made his England
debut aged 34, and became an unlikely hero.

JOHN ARLOTT: His white hair, he's prematurely
grey, showing quite strikingly under the cap. He
plays in glasses, a good sticker with some punishing
strokes, especially in front of the wicket. He tends
rather to play off the front foot ... that didn't do
Tom Graveney any harm but it's not always an asset
against bowlers of this pace. He's elder brother of
John Steele of Leicestershire and cousin of Brian
Crump who used to, like himself, play for Northants.
All three of them come from Staffordshire, that
richest of minor counties. Steele then a little over
average height – he's filled out in the last few years ...
he's fairly firmly built with square shoulders, a serious
man, takes a slightly crouching stance, bat barely
touching the ground as it rocks like a pendulum as
Lillee comes in, bowls to him, and he moves across
and lets that go outside the off stump ...

England v Australia, Lord's, July 1975

• • •

TREVOR BAILEY: And though Brian [Johnston] and myself may be getting a little bit weary of this massacre in the sun, it's a wonderful afternoon for Bill Frindall who is having an absolute ball because statistics are going left, right and centre. It's a great afternoon for the statisticians.

BRIAN JOHNSTON: You can hear the sparks coming out of his ears with the excitement.

England v West Indies, The Oval, August 1976

JOHN ARLOTT: On the whole, England's openings have not been impressive … Malone to Boycott, he gets that one away, wide of Thomson at mid-on for a single. And he takes the lead from Brearley by 39 to 37. And this at the moment bears close resemblance to a pursuit of my youth which was known as the 'Slow Bicycle Race', and the winner was the last one to cross the finishing line. I must say, these two are not so much neck and neck as bottom to bottom.

England v Australia, The Oval, August 1977

• • •

Geoff Boycott had just been recalled to the England side after a lengthy, self-imposed absence …

JOHN ARLOTT: Thomson comes in, bowls to Boycott. Boycott pushes back … there must be a run out here! Oh, how tragic … how tragic, how tragic, how tragic. We welcome World Service with the news that Randall has just this minute been sacrificially run out and England are 52 for 3 …

Randall almost with tears in his eyes. He looks very disconsolate.

England v Australia, Trent Bridge, July 1977

• • •

TONY COZIER: Dilley again comes in now to Richards. Short, and Richards hooks. It's going to be … it's gone out of the ground, I think. It's gone right over the Kensington Stand and even at that he seemed to hit it with one hand. Short ball, and Richards got under it and lifted it right over the top of the Kensington Stand and it finished up in a building site outside the ground. It was on its way to the deep-water harbour, but there are a few buildings in the way.

West Indies v England, Barbados, March 1981

• • •

HENRY BLOFELD: Although we are in the dying moments of the match, England 170 for 7, still 57 runs behind, we are seeing some attractive cricket. Both Botham, who is 34, and Dilley, who is 24, are putting bat to ball and runs are coming at quite a speed and in very entertaining fashion.

FRED TRUEMAN: The Australian bowlers, who have been in command for so long – suddenly, they do not really know where to bowl because the stick is being dished out. They are bowling a bit wide and giving Dilley a lot of room and he is liking that. It is giving him the chance to swing that bat and when he middles it, doesn't it go?

Later that day, when Botham left the field on 149 not out …

TREVOR BAILEY: It's the sort of innings which any great player would have been proud to play, including the likes of Sobers … It was a stupendous innings.

England v Australia, Headingley, July 1981

• • •

CHRISTOPHER MARTIN JENKINS: What a scene
is set now, because we've got two of the greatest of
all modern West Indies batsmen, Clive Lloyd
coming out to join Viv Richards with their side
in trouble – a full Lord's, sun shining. You really
couldn't ask for a situation more pregnant with
possibilities than that.

England v West Indies, Lord's, June 1984

• • •

*Malcolm Marshall had broken his wrist in the field but
still came out to bat for the West Indies at number 11,
his left arm in plaster.*

DON MOSEY: And here's Allott bowling to complete
his over, bowling to the one-handed Marshall who
gets runs, through the gully and Terry in pursuit. I
don't think he'll beat that to the ropes. Some helpful
youngster comes in, picks it up as it hits the ropes, lobs
it back and Marshall is off the mark with four runs
and Allott stands with his head downcast as much as

to say, 'Why can't I get out a man who's batting one-handed?'

England v West Indies, Headingley, July 1984

· · ·

Viv Richards had just scored the fastest century in Test cricket history, off only 56 balls.

CHRISTOPHER MARTIN JENKINS: The police come out to try to stop the spectators, but they can't do so and one gentleman in a blue shirt tries to lift him off the ground. The police trying to protect the uncrowned king of Antigua at the end of what has been an absolutely brilliant hundred.

West Indies v England, Antigua, April 1986

· · ·

FRED TRUEMAN (*on another English batting collapse*): It is unbelievable. All you want is someone out there with a top hat and tails and a big whip and get the elephants moving and we're in business. It is un-be-lievable.

Date unknown

• • •

David Gower was in the commentary box, having been controversially omitted from the touring party.

DAVID GOWER: That was a marvellous innings from Allan Lamb. Certainly worthy of a bottle of Bollinger – if he can find one in Kingston tonight.

West Indies v England, Jamaica, February 1990

• • •

Michael Atherton was on 97, just three away from a first Test century at Lord's.

BRIAN JOHNSTON: Atherton waits while Border comes up to bowl to him, and he flicks that one away and that may be it! Hughes is going to cut it off, is he? Yes, he's going to cut it off, down at midwicket, they've run two and they're going for the third! No! He's going to be run out! He is run out, oh! Atherton is run out! Sent back by Gatting, stranded, Merv Hughes throws and he is run out now for 99. And he's coming back, helmet off – that was a disaster for England …

England v Australia, Lord's, June 1994

• • •

VIV RICHARDS: I'm going to tell you something. This little sequence is going to be very interesting.

HENRY BLOFELD: Banks to Flintoff … Banks, the tall figure coming in now from the Pavilion End, bowls, it's short, Flintoff's down the wicket and he hits this with tremendous power and it goes for six, right down into the sightscreen beneath us. He came down the wicket to a long hop, hit it with a flat bat … that's his 150. He's 154 now and it's 507 for 7 and Vivian Richards read that one absolutely right.

VR: Well, this script was written in some huge, huge letters. Banks to Flintoff in this sort of mood … oh, I wouldn't like to be in Banks's position.

HB: No. I don't think Banks likes to be in it either.

England v West Indies, Edgbaston, July 2004

• • •

CHRISTOPHER MARTIN JENKINS: Here comes Lee into Pietersen … and he hooks that hard … oh, that's a great shot. That's the best of his sixes, because that went to a distant, old-fashioned Oval boundary. Down towards the block of flats opposite the Harleyford Road, just to the left of the pub at midwicket, right out of the meat of the bat.

Later that day …

JIM MAXWELL: Warne in to bowl and Pietersen swings into this and *mows* the ball away.

England v Australia, The Oval, September 2005

• • •

Like an elephant trying to do the pole vault.

JONATHAN AGNEW after Pakistan skipper Inzamam-ul-Haq was out, in ungainly fashion, hit wicket.

England v Pakistan, Headingley, August 2006

• • •

SIMON MANN: You must have put a few spectators to sleep in your time, Geoffrey?

GEOFF BOYCOTT: Yeah, but I were still battin' when they woke up!

Sri Lanka v England, 2011

JONATHAN AGNEW: Broad's out! He's out, he flicked that away to slip … I think. It's been taken by Clarke and they're appealing. And Aleem Dar … hang on, Aleem Dar is saying not out. Australia have got no reviews left. Broad's leaning on his bat. That looked to me as if he edged it straight to slip. And Aleem Dar's saying not out. And the Australians are furious! Absolutely furious!

GEOFF BOYCOTT (*laughing*): You've got no reviews left, lads!

JA: I don't blame Australia for being really, really narked about that. For goodness' sake, that's out anywhere you want. It's disappointing, I must say, to see someone standing for that. But Broad is not walking. He's stood there and there are no reviews left. That's another ridiculous one.

England v Australia, Trent Bridge, July 2013

• • •

England's substandard batting in the 5-0 Ashes defeat during the winter of 2013/2014 drew some scathing and colourful criticism from Geoff Boycott …

GEOFF BOYCOTT: It's not a good morning. It's a pathetic display of batting …

GEOFF BOYCOTT:

Well, it's stupid. There's more brains in a pork pie, isn't there?

GEOFF BOYCOTT: If I were you in England I'd go to sleep. Because this could become a nightmare. This has been a shocker this morning.

GEOFF BOYCOTT: That was like my mum hanging out the washing.

GEOFF BOYCOTT (*after Joe Root was out to a rash shot*): More brains in a chocolate mousse.

Australia v England, 2013/14

• • •

GRAEME SWANN: Moeen Ali is a natural timer of the ball and quite wristy. When he hits the ball, it makes a crack like a rifle shot. He's also beautiful off his legs, through the covers. It's just so easy. I'm going to call him the bearded Gower from now on …

England v Sri Lanka, Headingley, June 2014

Champagne Moments

REX ALSTON: And here's the applause for Bradman as he comes in. Well, it's a wonderful reception. The whole crowd is standing and the England team are joining in – led by Yardley – three cheers for the Don, as he gets to the wicket.

And now the crowd settles down again … 40 minutes left for play and Bradman is now taking guard. Hollies is going to bowl at him and John Arlott shall describe the first ball. So come on, John…

JOHN ARLOTT: Well, I don't think I'm as deadly as you are Rex [*Alston had just described a wicket*

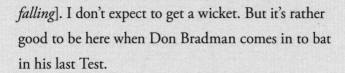

falling]. I don't expect to get a wicket. But it's rather good to be here when Don Bradman comes in to bat in his last Test.

And now here's Hollies to bowl to him from the Vauxhall End. He bowls, and Bradman goes back across his wicket and pushes the ball gently in the direction of the Houses of Parliament, which are out beyond silly mid-off. It doesn't go that far, it merely goes to Watkins at silly mid-off. No run. Still 117 for 1.

Two slips, a silly mid-off and forward short leg close to him as Hollies pitches the ball up slowly and … he's bowled! Bradman bowled Hollies nought. Bowled Hollies, nought [*Arlott pauses as Bradman walks back to the pavilion*].

And, what do you say under those circumstances? I wonder if you see the ball very clearly in your last Test in England? On a ground where you've played some of the biggest cricket of your life and where the opposing side has just stood around you and given you three cheers, and the crowd has clapped you all the way to the wicket – I wonder if you really see the ball at all?

England v Australia, The Oval, August 1948

• • •

REX ALSTON (*the West Indies had just won their first ever Test match in England*): There are one or two West Indian characters coming out on the field, waving their hats as the West Indies players walk quietly off the field. Yes, there are several West Indian supporters running from the far end and they are going to escort their team off the field. The score is 274.

Goddard running in with his stump, being chased harum-scarum by lots of West Indian supporters. Such a sight never been seen before at Lord's.

England v West Indies, Lord's, June 1950

PIGEONS, BUSES, RAIN AND CRANES

Test Match Special has always been about more than the cricket. Often, in between balls, the commentator's eye is taken by something unusual, whether that's in the stands, on the outfield, in the sky, or the roads around the ground. There have also been endless breaks for rain and bad light, during which TMS *often comes into its own.*

REX ALSTON: Now he's holding the play up for something unusual. It looks like a mouse running across the field! Is it? It's gone to Dexter who's picking it up. Yes, it looks like a mouse. Yes, it's run up to the stumps now … Well, that's quite an invasion. Looks rather a big mouse … Mouse Stopped Play.

England v Pakistan, Lord's, June 1962

JOHN ARLOTT (*on Clive Lloyd's hundred*): And the whole crowd seething with West Indian delight. I can only say it was worth this; it was worth the treatment it's getting. I thought I saw a policeman applauding.

Australia v West Indies, World Cup final, Lord's, June 1975

• • •

TONY COZIER: The West Indies have declared and Tony Greig has gone on his hands and knees and to the delight of the West Indies spectators, now smiling all over his face, gone on his hands and knees and for three or four paces has, in his own words, 'grovelled' in front of the West Indian spectators … That was a good little touch by Tony Greig and I think the West Indian supporters appreciated it.

England v West Indies, The Oval, August 1976

• • •

JOHN ARLOTT: The other hazard at the moment is
a colony of silver gulls, several hundreds of them. At
first they pitched on the top of the stand as if they
were vultures recruited for Lillee …

Australia v England, Melbourne, March 1977

• • •

I can see
a butterfly
walking
across the
pitch, and
what's more it
appears to
have a limp.

HENRY BLOFELD

. . .

CHRISTOPHER MARTIN JENKINS: The sun beginning to get just a bit lower, the shadows lengthen to almost the same size as the men who are throwing them.

Date unknown

• • •

On hearing a loud voice in the crowd …

JOHN ARLOTT: We've got a beauty of a loudmouth over in the Mound Stand now, talking pure alcohol. Hear that? Worse than the Sydney Hill but fewer in number. 95 for 2.

England v Pakistan, Lord's, June 1978

• • •

HENRY BLOFELD: Oh look, another claret-coloured bus. I love these claret-coloured buses. They give me all sorts of ideas …

England v India, Trent Bridge, August 2002

• • •

BRIAN JOHNSTON: The pigeons have shifted now to behind mid-on. I don't know who gives the signal, when they've consumed the number of … I don't think it's worms, I think it's seeds they go for … You think pigeons don't eat worms? … They must do?

BILL FRINDALL: I think someone wrote in and said they're not carnivorous.

BJ: Which means they wouldn't eat worms. I bet if I offered a worm to a pigeon he would eat it. Would you get one for me? One of Blowers' thoughtful looking pigeons … we'll offer it a worm. I bet it would eat it.

Date unknown

• • •

Brian Johnston was a fan of the daytime soap opera
Neighbours ...

BRIAN JOHNSTON: Oh, a bit of bad news. Nick
in *Neighbours* has sprained his ankle falling off his
skateboard. Oh dear, well these things do happen.
Here's Kapil Dev ...

BILL FRINDALL: How many people in the cast of
Neighbours?

BJ: About 12, active ones.

BF: One down, 11 to go then.

BJ: He'll be all right, old Nick. He couldn't go in
the race and Matt took his place and I haven't seen if
he won.

UNKNOWN: Do you really watch that programme, BJ?

BJ: Yes … and a friend of mine overlooking Green Park is putting every single one down on video for me for when I get back. There's been a lot of events going on there. Jim's tree was cut down, that was the trouble.

UNKNOWN: I don't know what you're talking about.

BJ: A lot of people do listen to it. It's a very serious programme.

UNKNOWN: Do you watch *Coronation Street* as well?

BJ: No no no, I only watch *Neighbours*. But when one's at a Test match one can't do it. I'm delighted to be at the Test but I like a report day-by-day …

England v India, 1990

• • •

HENRY BLOFELD: A policeman comes tripping down the grandstand balcony there, coming down the steps at the double. Now he's walking on to the scaffolding. I don't know what he's doing. Rather urgently he's walking … [*he commentates on play*] … Our policeman is still perambulating at some speed. He's just passed another cover, three members of the groundstaff, a television crew and a tractor. Now he looks like he's got some very definite object in view … [*he commentates on another passage of play*] … Our policeman did reappear then and walked off, left-right-left, very formidable, behind the sightscreen. PC 49 we might get him on the right-hand … there he is, he's appeared – how exciting! He's passing some colleagues sitting on a bench there – doesn't even give them a look. Here comes Jones, bowls and Lamb uses his feet and drives for four. Hadlee dives to his left at mid-off and can't get to it. And the policeman … Look! It's bobbled over the rope and the policeman has gone under the tarpaulin there, he's taken his helmet off and he's fielded the ball!

What a splendid journey our bobby's had. Do you
think he's enjoyed it?

England v New Zealand, Lord's, June 1990

• • •

HENRY BLOFELD: A low-level pigeon goes past
almost hugging the ground, having a look at the
members in the pavilion. A lady in a bright orange
shirt walks up the seats there in the grandstand
balcony … she's got a large pigtail too …

Date unknown

• • •

HENRY BLOFELD: The first aeroplane of the season
has just disappeared behind the block of flats at the
far end of the ground, on its way towards Heathrow,
and Javed has a wild drive. He wasn't anywhere near
it I think, which is just as well for him as there are
four avaricious slips waiting for the edge …

Date unknown

• • •

HENRY BLOFELD: Oh, look, I've actually just seen a crane at Lord's moving, doing some work. I've seen cranes all round this ground for years and they've always been still. That white one there is moving … a moving crane, a yellow helicopter, what more has play got to offer?

BILL FRINDALL: Rain.

HB:

Bill, you're an eternal pessimist about this rain.

...

NEVILLE OLIVER: The City of Sheffield Centenary cake has just been carried in … by horse and dray. And Gooch defends away in the off side and there's no run. Can you really lift that? You're a strong man. It's the biggest cake I've ever seen.

Date unknown

• • •

The final afternoon's play was abandoned as the result of a dramatic storm, at which Henry Blofeld gave one of his most vivid commentaries …

HENRY BLOFELD: Looking at the stand to our right people are huddled up against the back of the stand [*loud crash of thunder*] and the thunder and the lightning, you can hear it in the sound effects … When you look to our left, there's a half-built stand, the girders are there like scaffolding, it really does look like a bomb has [*enormous crash of thunder*] … ooh, and there's another one. Now you look out on the ground and before long it's going to be under water. Down on the right-hand side there are great long pools of water inside the boundary rope and the rain is sweeping in great drifts across the ground. There are terrific puddles at the far end. I can't see in front of the hill there because there simply isn't any light at all.

VIC MARKS: Double wipers weather, isn't it, Henry?

HB: Oh, yes, it is. It's absolutely amazing and I wouldn't have missed this for the world.

Australia v England, Brisbane, November 1998

• • •

PIGEONS, BUSES, RAIN AND CRANES   47

CHRISTOPHER MARTIN JENKINS: Well, as it's raining, I'll read you the full regulations – see if you can understand it. 'Play shall continue on each day until the completion of the minimum number of overs. On days other than the last day, a minimum number of 90. On the last day, a minimum of 75 or 15 overs an hour, er, other than the last hour when clause five below shall apply.' And clause five below says [*nervous laugh*], I'm going to thoroughly confuse you now, 'Laws 17.6 and 17.7 will apply. Except that a minimum of 15 six-ball overs shall be bowled in the last hour.' In other words, this is nothing to do with the rain at the moment, er, on the last day now they are having 15, not 20 overs in the last hour … 'If at any time after 30 minutes of the last hour have elapsed, both captains accept there is no prospect of a result to the match they may agree to cease play at that time …'

ASIF IQBAL: Right, which means that at half past five, if they agree to call it off, you can. You don't have to go on for one hour …

CMJ: Yes, that's right [*laughter in the background*]. But there is a new ruling on the additional hour [*laughs*].

AI: Which is?

CMJ: 'Except in the last hour of the match …' [*laughs*] Excuse me, 'in the event of play being suspended for any reason other than normal intervals' [*pauses*] … 'the playing time on that day shall be' [*laughs*] I'm sorry … there's mirth at this. These regulations can always cause a little confusion …

AI: That's the reason I'm asking you and I'm sure the listeners would also like to know.

CMJ (*reads again*): 'The playing time shall be extended by the amount of time lost, up to a maximum of an hour.' In other words you can have an additional hour …

AI: I see …

CMJ: I think that Alan Curtis was telling me earlier today that that applied on the last day as well …

AI: Right, but I think as we see now there's every likelihood it may not apply here because the sun is out and they are taking the covers back so hopefully we don't have to go into it and confuse ourselves as well as the listeners.

CMJ: Well, that's a great relief to us all, certainly. It was a very brief shower and the sun is now brightly out and I hope everyone at home is now completely understanding of the crystal-clear regulations which I read out. 421 for 6 is the score and we have succeeded in reducing even Asif Iqbal to giggles.

DAVID LLOYD: He's just left. He's enquiring what day it is …

CMJ: Well, I think it's Monday.

England v India, 1990

• • •

HENRY BLOFELD: And a rather portly gentleman in yellow – or would you call that orange, Foxy [Graeme Fowler]? – chemise is getting an enormous cheer. He's a carrying a tray with five, no, six pints of beer. I dare say he'll be very popular when he finally arrives at his destination. And, yes, well, jolly good luck to you, sir.

Date unknown

• • •

JONATHAN AGNEW: A vicious-looking insect appears on our window here. We're used to seeing flies, maybe the odd wasp in a commentary box, but I hate to think what that is.

BARRY RICHARDS: It's a monster, isn't it?

JA: Not sure what it is.

BR: He's on the outside, Aggers, don't panic.

JA: That's all right, I'm just checking the area is completely sealed. I think it is. We don't want that flying around in here … it's got six legs, must be at least an inch long, with these enormous antennae … This is played off the front foot by Kallis up to short extra cover and there's no run.

South Africa v England, World Cup, Guyana, March 2007

• • •

CHRISTOPHER MARTIN JENKINS: The horrible sight of a rather obese Englishman in what appeared to be underpants, but are very, very short shorts indeed. Anyway, that was on the television …

Date unknown

• • •

BRIAN JOHNSTON: A streaker has arrived … a very, very obvious streaker. He's running on and he is holding some kind of hat in his hand. He has socks and shoes on and I don't know what he's going to do when he gets to the stumps … nothing. He's talking to Jack Russell and he's got his gloves on. The umpires don't quite know what to do. He's going to trot off, making a dignified trot across to the square-leg umpire. I don't think he's been sunbathing much – he's bit lighter down the backside than the rest of his body. And he risks … oof … he climbed over the board, and it was higher than he thought and it was a little bit painful for him I think. You heard the ooh from the crowd …

Date unknown

Champagne Moments

BERNARD KERR: Morris with his face wreathed in smiles, sends up one to Compton short outside leg stump. Compton hooks and there's the Ashes! England have won as the ball crashes to the boundary. Two wickets down for 132, with Compton not out 22 and Edrich not out 55. Congratulations England on regaining the Ashes, and now the crowd are absolutely swarming the ground, they're coming across like ants, thousands and thousands of people ... I can see Denis Compton and Bill Edrich being embraced, being kissed by girls and women. I think they'll be bruised by the time they get in. People are now assembled in front of the broadcasting box as this thick crowd forms a lane for the players to make their way to the pavilion.

This is staggering, highly exciting. As a matter of fact, it's rather moving. From the broadcasting box, you can't see any grass at all – there's just a whole carpet of humanity. Now they're just standing still. I'm afraid they can't move at all – shoulder-to-shoulder, just as thick as can be. It really is just a wonderful sight.

England v Australia, The Oval, August 1953

• • •

JOHN ARLOTT: Old Trafford has redeemed itself with a last hour of flawless sunshine. Laker comes in again, hair flopping, bowls to Maddocks, it turns and Laker appeals – and he's out lbw and Laker's taken all ten!

The first man to congratulate him is Ian Johnson. And England have won by an innings and 170 and

Laker has taken all ten wickets for 53 in the second innings … and there are friends of mine who were not going to come today. They thought it would rain. Well, it did look as if it was going to rain. They missed a very great piece of bowling.

England v Australia, Old Trafford, July 1956

DEMON
BOWLING

South African bowler Norman 'Tufty' Mann was causing England captain George Mann some problems with the ball.

JOHN ARLOTT:

What we have here is a clear case of Mann's inhumanity to Mann.

England v South Africa, Johannesburg, December 1947

• • •

JOHN ARLOTT: And Trueman comes in, bowls to Miller, Miller gropes and Evans has caught most gloriously! And now all round the ground, the entire crowd standing to this man again [*Miller had earlier taken 5 for 72*]. Well, with two receptions like that – three in fact – in one day at Lord's, Miller should go to bed tonight a happy man. Men have made more than 30 runs in Tests here but not so many of them have made them as handsomely as that. 112 for 6, Miller caught Evans bowled Trueman. And Trueman, after a few years in the wilderness as a Test fast bowler, back right in the picture with 4 for 35, and four wickets as good as those of Burke, Harvey, Burge and Miller. What a good bag!

England v Australia, Lord's, June 1956

· · ·

JOHN ARLOTT (*on Peter Loader's hat-trick*): He's bowled him all over the place, it's a hat-trick, and Loader is jumping all over the place like a monkey on a stick.

England v West Indies, Headingley, July 1957

· · ·

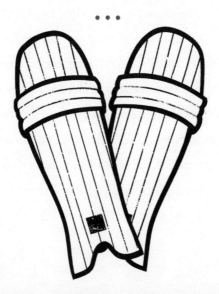

He reminds me of Groucho Marx chasing a pretty waitress.

JOHN ARLOTT on Asif Masood's distinctive bowling action.

England v Pakistan, 1971

• • •

JOHN ARLOTT: [Ken] Higgs back on his little semi-circular walk. Little scuffle of the feet, a few stalking, walking strides and he's in to bowl …

Date unknown

• • •

JOHN ARLOTT (*on Eddie Barlow's hat-trick*): The ball comes back to him, he turns and walks back, his shirt out at the back, broad-backed, strong looking, stocky, he comes in, bowls to Knott and bowls him … spreads his stumps like twigs. 219 for 7 …

They all get down and in comes Barlow to Wilson, he bowls to him, he goes forward, the ball pops up and he's caught … he's caught at forward short leg! And Barlow is poised in altogether different melodramatic pose which says 'Done it at last'. And he's got his hat-trick. Well, I've only ever seen two Test hat-tricks in my life. They were both on this same ground and both about the same time of day.

England v Rest of the World, Headingley, July 1970

• • •

BRIAN JOHNSTON: A few moments ago, Snow bowled a short ball which hit Jenner on the head. It knocked him down, he was taken off to tremendous boos and the result was that another batsman came in. Snow finished the over. Some words passed between him and Lou Rowan. Lou Rowan said something to the other umpire. It could have been a warning for bumpers. It could have been something which Snow said.

Snow then came down to the hill below us here. Beer cans were thrown, not necessarily at him but

they were thrown in the area where he was fielding, and Illingworth then called him up but Snow came back down here. Someone shook him by the hand in the crowd and patted him on the back, but then there was another hail of cans thrown at him. They're also being thrown at the far end of the hill. The groundsman, Athol Watkins, is going out to collect some of them and when Snow came down here they bombarded him with cans. Illingworth came down with half his team, said something to Snow and he's led them off the field. It's an unprecedented position, this.

Australia v England, Sydney, February 1971

• • •

HENRY BLOFELD: He walks back, looks at the ball as though it's about to explode. It doesn't. He bowls and there's no run.

Date unknown

• • •

HENRY BLOFELD: Holding walks slowly back into the distance. Now here he is … he certainly runs in at absolutely breakneck speed. He's up past [umpire] Alley, he bowls and … oooh, that's another short one, Close backs away as it flies past his shirt buttons. Well, that's two in a row and I'm quite certain, in a way, though he can't exactly be enjoying it, Close … well a part of him will be relishing this. He loves a fight and there's no one better equipped to take these fast bowlers on than Brian Close. Even at the age of 45 … Here's Holding again, he's racing in, he bowls to Close, that's a short one, he takes it on the body … and even Brian Close is staggering after that one! He buckled at the knees for a moment, and seeing this John Edrich comes down the wicket to talk to him … dear old Brian Close, he's still not rubbing anything. He's looking quite unconcerned now, joining with Edrich, talking, patting down the wicket … I think in fact, having been hit in the side by that one, he slightly lost his balance as he moved over to the off side. I would think that was probably the reason, wouldn't you, Fred?

FRED TRUEMAN: I don't know. I think it hurt the old boy. He buckled a little at the knees. It was a nasty one … and when you can see where they're patting down, it wasn't all that short. It came up, didn't it?

HB:

Yes, it did. And still Close has not rubbed any part of him. What an amazing man he is …

England v West Indies, Old Trafford, July 1976

• • •

JOHN ARLOTT: About six feet tall with quite a good pair of shoulders, but a lithe man rather than a heavyweight. Holding comes up like the sprinter he once was, high on his toes, lovely smooth approach …

Later in that match …

BRIAN JOHNSTON (*Tony Greig had just been dismissed*): Well, Fred, what about that one? It's a sad thing for Tony Greig.

FRED TRUEMAN: It's a sad thing for Tony Greig but what a magnificent delivery by Holding. He knows this high backlift of Greig's, which they've played on, and he came up, first delivery, and bowled *the perfect yorker* on the leg stump and knocked the leg stump right outta the ground, leaving Tony Greig completely nonplussed.

England v West Indies, The Oval, August 1976

• • •

JOHN ARLOTT: Vincent Van Der Bijl, bald pate gleaming in the sun … looking remarkably like Lord Longford, but not nearly so tolerant.

Date unknown

• • •

JOHN ARLOTT: Consider Lillee in the field. He toils, but he does not spin.

Date unknown

• • •

BRIAN JOHNSTON: He's [Bob Willis] coming in now to bowl to Haynes … and Haynes is hit on the pad, that must be lbw! He's got him lbw. That looked absolutely plummers …

England v West Indies, Edgbaston, June 1984

• • •

And he's bowled him! Cleaners! Middle stump absolutely knocked out.

BRIAN JOHNSTON
England v West Indies, 1988

...

Malcolm Marshall had broken his wrist in the field, but that didn't stop him destroying England with the ball.

TONY COZIER: So the first time that Malcolm Marshall has taken seven wickets in an innings and what a performance by the one-armed bandit …

England v West Indies, Headingley, July 1984

• • •

BRIAN JOHNSTON: So here's Ellison, Edmonds is very close in now on the leg side … and he's out, he's bowled! Border is bowled by Ellison, 36 for 5 Australia, Border bowled Ellison for two, ten wickets in the match for Ellison so far, and the England team are cock-a-hoop.

England v Australia, Edgbaston, August 1985

• • •

DON MOSEY: Here's Walsh bowling to Cowdrey, who's bowled! Beaten for pace off the pitch, late on it and the middle stump sagged drunkenly backwards …

England v West Indies, Headingley, July 1988

• • •

CHRISTOPHER MARTIN JENKINS: And Patterson, I can reveal, by courtesy of Tony Cozier, is bowling in a box. I've known of no other bowler in the history of cricket who's bowled in a box and I'll tell you why in a moment … The reason is that he follows through with his right arm and sometimes hits himself in a painful place.

England v West Indies, 1988

• • •

BRIAN JOHNSTON: Fred, who do you think were the six fastest bowlers since the war?

FRED TRUEMAN: There were me …

BJ: Oh, there must have been seven.

Date unknown

• • •

Quick? I could bowl quicker in me mac.

FRED TRUEMAN on Darren Gough.

England v South Africa, 1994

• • •

HENRY BLOFELD: Here's Caddick, he's in now and he bowls, McMillan drives and Caddick catches him! He's caught and bowled! Caddick took a wicket with his first ball and he stands there with his arms outstretched as if to say 'Anyone can do it. Look, it's the easiest thing in the world!' He held out his hands like a conjurer after doing a good trick.

New Zealand v England, Christchurch, March 2002

• • •

VIC MARKS: They switched ends, which is always a good ploy if the game has gone to sleep. I reckon they've switched ends to get different umpires on.

JONATHAN AGNEW: You're a canny old so-and-so, aren't you, Victor? In goes Giles, there's no stroke played … and he's given him out! That's exactly right, Victor. Daryl Hair has a record for giving batsmen out for not playing a shot outside the off stump and in Daryl Hair's mind that was precisely what Chanderpaul did there, though Chanderpaul looks most aggrieved as he walks off. And umpire Hair has given him out leg before wicket. Victor,

I hate to say this, but for once in your life you are ahead of the game …

England v West Indies, Edgbaston, August 2004

• • •

JONATHAN AGNEW: Harmison from the far end, bowls the first ball of the series … oh, my word, it's gone straight to second slip! What a horrible start! I can't believe I've seen it.

VIC MARKS: It went straight to Freddie Flintoff who did well to stop it, frankly. Talk about setting the tone … we'll remember that delivery for a long time, I'm afraid, if this proves to be one of England's unsuccessful campaigns down under … [*England were to lose the series 5-0*].

JA: That is just about the worst delivery I've ever seen in Test cricket.

Australia v England, Brisbane, November 2006

• • •

Matt Prior had just been comprehensively bowled by
Australia's Mitchell Johnson.

PHIL TUFNELL:

He's been feng shui'd.

CHRISTOPHER MARTIN JENKINS: What do you mean, feng shui'd?

PT:

He's had his furniture rearranged.

England v Australia, Lord's, July 2009

. . .

GEOFF BOYCOTT: He's knocked the middle pole down first ball! Jimmy Anderson, you're gone, you're gone … you can get off now, the Ashes have gone. Forget this match, they've flown away.

Australia v England, Adelaide, December 2013

Champagne Moments

JOHN ARLOTT (*Fred Trueman needed only one more wicket to become the first bowler to take 300 Test match wickets*): Trueman with a bit of a scowl at the batsman. Doesn't even look friendly towards his fieldsmen at the moment. In his 31st over. He has two wickets, wants a third. Trueman in again, bowls to Hawke and Hawke goes forward and is caught. There's the 300th! … There was no nicer touch than Trueman congratulating Hawke. Caught by Cowdrey. Neil Hawke can never have come into the pavilion to a greater ovation in his life but they weren't looking at him. Fred Trueman's 300th

Test wicket. The first man in the history of cricket
to achieve the figure, when Hawke played a half-
hearted stroke outside the off stump to a ball that
took the outside edge and Cowdrey swooped on it,
two hands … Up went Trueman, up went the crowd,
[they] stood to him, cheered him and as Hawke
walked away Trueman congratulated him.

England v Australia, The Oval, August 1964

• • •

*After torrential rain on the final day, The Oval crowd
had helped mop the pitch to give England a chance of
victory and the opportunity to square the series. With
only ten minutes of play left, the Australians were nine
wickets down …*

JOHN ARLOTT: Underwood hammering away,
bustling back to his mark, tossing the ball from
hand to hand, nervous strain on both sides now.
A situation in which a bowler could press too much.
Underwood comes in, bowls and he has padded

away, and he is out! Played deliberately with his pad, Inverarity. Just missed carrying his bat to a ball that just about straightened.

England v Australia, The Oval, August 1968

COMMENTATORS
BEHAVING
BADLY

The following exchange was not transmitted but highlights Brian Johnston's impish sense of humour.

BRIAN JOHNSTON (*Tony Cozier enters the box after a rain break*): … well, those are the up-to-date statistics of the MCC team to the nearest decimal point, and you know all of their ages, dates of their birthday and their exact batting and bowling figures. Ah, I see Tony Cozier has just come into the box so I'll ask him to give you exactly the same information about the West Indies players. Tony …

TONY COZIER: [*pause*] Well, Brian, I'll try to tell the listeners in a moment, but perhaps you'd like to hear about the state of the pitch, which I've just passed on my way back?

BJ: No, sorry, Tony. We talked about it whilst you were away. All we want – and straight away, please – is the information about the West Indian statistics.

TC: [*silence*]

BJ: Well, Tony, if you can't give us the details
I suppose we had better return to the studio.
So goodbye from us all here.

West Indies v England, Trinidad, March 1968

• • •

JOHN ARLOTT: Well, if you're awake in England, it's
worth staying awake still, I reckon. Take a sickie in
the morning.

Australia v England, Melbourne, March 1977

• • •

Cunis, a funny sort of name: neither one thing nor the other.

JOHN ARLOTT

. . .

BRIAN JOHNSTON: Olly [*Colin Milburn's nickname*], what did you think of that last stroke?

COLIN MILBURN: [*pause*] Very good shot. [*Laughter in the box*] I enjoyed it. Alan Lamb takes ... er, you're just trying to do me because I've got a mouthful of cake.

BJ: Yes, you have, and you're spitting it all into the microphone too. Really, Olly, in the middle of the over, you can't resist the cream puffs …

England v West Indies, 1988

• • •

John Arlott had been commentating on a county match with a young commentator who was keen to impress the old master with his poetic turn of phrase. Sadly, this only consisted of one sentence: 'The sun is sinking slowly in the west.' Arlott became increasingly exasperated ...

JOHN ARLOTT: He comes in to bowl. And, by the way, over his right shoulder the sun is still sinking slowly in the west. If by chance it should start to sink anywhere else, we'll be the first to let you know ...

Date unknown

• • •

Sometimes the modern world was a mystery to Fred Trueman ... that included the difference between a mobile phone and a walkie-talkie.

CHRISTOPHER MARTIN JENKINS: The umpires are now using their walkie-talkies. For some reason the ICC seem hell-bent on abandoning the use of walkie-talkies but it makes absolute sense for the umpires to communicate with people, whoever it might be, and this is just one classic example.

FRED TRUEMAN: Well, they use 'em everywhere else, they might as well use 'em here.

CMJ: Well, they might as well …

FT: Every time I get on train they're ringing. Carrying on … oooh, it is annoyin'. At one time you used to be able to get on the train, have a cup of coffee, read the paper, close your eyes, have a little nap, and now there's telephones ringing, people making bids for this and making bids for that, ooh it does annoy me on that train. It's a shame, because the trains on the East Coast service are beautiful trains. They really are. I don't want to hear people saying, 'Oh I don't want to pay more than 200 and odd thousand for that, well I offered them £300,000 a few weeks ago, no I don't think it's worth that now.' I don't want to know!

Date unknown

• • •

CHRISTOPHER MARTIN JENKINS: Are you a golfer, Colin?

COLIN MILBURN: No, I'm not. I don't have the patience for that. It's a long way to walk before you have a pint …

England v West Indies, 1988

• • •

BRIAN JOHNSTON: I'm joined by Olly Milburn, if you heard the shaking box. He just landed in the seat beside me …

England v West Indies, 1988

• • •

BRIAN JOHNSTON: We've often asked Fred what he thought of as he walked back and it was an Australian Prime Minister who said you were uttering Greek Iambics to yourself or something. Didn't he? Mr Menzies?

FRED TRUEMAN: Oh, Robert? He was a great man.

BJ: Sir Robert.

FT:

Well, he became Sir Robert, but if you called him Sir he gave you a right telling off.

BJ: Did he?

FT: Oh sure.

BJ: Great man. Another maiden from Dilley and after a word from you I think we'll have the Alderman shall we?

FT: Yes, but, er, just before you go, Sir Robert Menzies, you're quite right ... I said to him, because I've been a friend of his for years, he was so marvellous ... when he bought me that silver tankard for my birthday and presented it to me in Canberra when we played cricket there ... For the Prime Minister of Australia to know it was my birthday was absolutely remarkable.

BJ: Well, he was amazed when I rang him up to tell him beforehand.

Date unknown

• • •

CHRISTOPHER MARTIN JENKINS: Tait bowls to the right-handed Kevin O'Brien, a yorker which he turns for three … it might have the legs to go all the way for four, it's touch and go … it's made it. Just bobbled over the ropes.

VIC MARKS: I have played cricket with you, CMJ, but I'm eternally grateful I never had to run between the wickets with you very often.

CMJ: I practically never get it wrong. You would have said no, would you? You would have held your hand up and refused to run?

VM: No, I would have stood on my bat handle, in that particular instance.

CMJ: Well, you were a very arrogant player, Vic …

Australia v Ireland, Barbados, World Cup, April 2007

• • •

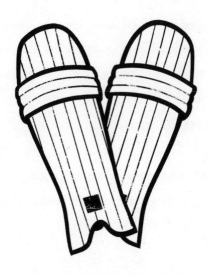

News of Lily Allen's imminent arrival in the TMS *box for 'View from the Boundary' interview had failed to reach Phil Tufnell …*

JONATHAN AGNEW: Don't you know? Oh, Tuffers, where have you been? It's someone who travelled on a bus from Amsterdam to be here.

PHIL TUFNELL: Dennis Bergkamp?

England v Australia, The Oval, August 2009

• • •

*After England won the Ashes, Jonathan Agnew
performed the 'Sprinkler', a 'dance' the England team
had introduced during the tour.*

VIC MARKS: He's taking off his accreditation.
He's there in his pink shirt. And he goes! He goes!
He's swinging his arms around. He's looking a mere
62 as he does it. He's done it three times, there's a
ripple of applause ...

PHOTOGRAPHER: That was awful.

VM: That's one of our snappers, who's a very objective
sort of chap.

Australia v England, Sydney, January 2011

• • •

JONATHAN AGNEW: Are you still having to take all those tablets, Geoffrey?

GEOFF BOYCOTT: Aye. Lots of vitamins and things. These ones are cyanide, actually.

JA: Really? You don't fancy doing us all a favour and taking a few more of them, do you?

Date unknown

• • •

JONATHAN AGNEW: Who was your sporting hero? Whose photo was on your bedroom wall? Mine was Geoffrey Boycott. Who was yours?

PHIL TUFNELL: Linda Lusardi.

India v England, November 2012

• • •

JONATHAN AGNEW: Blowers has returned. There's a full page of Blowers in the fashion area of one of today's more respectable, if that's the right word, newspapers. And he's there, and splendid he looks …

PHIL TUFNELL: Is it *The Times* or the *Telegraph*?

JA: Well, it's a broadsheet. Here it is, look at this … it's the *Telegraph Weekend*.

PT: A male model.

JA: He is a male model … 'Cricket buff and bon viveur Henry Blofeld knows a thing or two about sartorial finery' is how the article starts. 'And here are his favourites' … So there it is. What's he wearing? Actually, for Henry, the picture of Blowers – there's a younger model alongside him, I don't think that was Henry forty years ago – but Henry by his standards is quite conservatively dressed. Hands thrust casually into the pockets of his trousers, jacket …

PT: Cravat …

JA: Indeed. Of course he has a cravat.

PT: They've been making a comeback I've been told.

JA: … His article is a sort of a letter, an open letter to the readers. It starts, perhaps not surprisingly, 'My

Dear Old Things … I don't think I've ever been one
to rattle on about sartorial elegance. I simply like to
lead by example…' [*laughter*] And it goes downhill
from there, frankly. 'Being a modest chap, I don't
want to go over the top. But it was drummed into
me when I was young that it's not quite the done
thing to be too conscious of your appearance.'

PT: Just let it naturally happen.

JA: 'Nonetheless, you mustn't let the side down if
you're on parade.' There you go … he never lets
the side down. 'A dashing sock always catches the
eye…' [*laughter*] 'But the most important thing is
to come up with clothes that are comfortable to
wear. The trick is, buy the best and the clothes speak
for themselves.' … This is lovely stuff, Blowers is a
very fine dresser. 'It simply doesn't do to look like
a tailor's dummy with everything symmetrically in
place.' That would explain the odd problem with the
flies we've had. 'Take a handkerchief, for example.
I just flick my silk handkerchief open, tucked into
my top pocket, where I think it does the job with

something approaching aplomb.' That is aplomb not looking like a plum, though it's sometimes hard not to tell the difference. 'Ties are off the menu these days. I think a decently tied silk cravat lends a touch of class and bridges this gap pretty well ...' It's lovely stuff, dear old Blowers. You can read the article and see what Blowers is wearing today on the *Test Match Special* Facebook page ...

PT:

The Giorgio Armani of the commentary box ...

England v Australia, Lord's, July 2013

• • •

BBC Radio One DJ Greg James had paid a visit to the TMS *box and his appearance had not pleased Geoffrey Boycott.*

SIMON MANN: Now I hear, Geoffrey, that you've been unkind to that nice presenter from Radio One, Greg James … questioning his dress sense.

GEOFF BOYCOTT (*laughs*): Well, if you'd have seen it on television it would have been an eye-opener, let me tell you.

SM: You described him as the worst dressed presenter you've ever seen …

GB: Yeah. That's about right. He was.

SM: I'll put a picture out of his t-shirt on Twitter.

GB: Will you? I reckon it was a five-year-old with a crayon what's drawn that.

SM: Not very nice to say that on air, Geoffrey.

GB: Really? Well, it's the truth – you can say it.

SM: We don't always say the truth, Geoffrey.

GB: Why not? That's what's wrong with the country.

SM: I wouldn't want to offend you.

GB: Tell anything you want about me. I don't mind. Jonathan [Agnew] does it regularly. It doesn't seem to bother him, does it? He gives me some hokey-pokey all the time.

SM: That's just playful banter, though.

GB: Well, it was with him [Greg James]... did you see his shoes as well? Oh, blimey.

SM: I didn't take a picture of his shoes.

GB: He had jeans on. Jeans! ... working for the BBC at Test match in jeans. If he comes to Headingley for the one-day [match] he's not coming in the committee room. Because I'm President.

England v Australia, Old Trafford, August 2013

• • •

Greg James, despite his dressing down over his dress sense, recorded a message from pop singer Katy Perry for Geoffrey …

KATY PERRY (*recorded*): Hi, Geoffrey, it's Katy Perry. I think you're beautiful and your style is stunning. When I'm next in the UK you'll have to show me around the Yorkshire countryside.

GEOFF BOYCOTT: Katie, I'll show you anywhere. Definitely.

England v Australia, Durham, August 2013

• • •

A Babybel cheese was thrown on to the pitch during play ...

We'll have to get CSI Yorkshire to dust the cheese for prints ...

GRAEME SWANN

England v Sri Lanka, Headingley, June 2014

• • •

EBONY RAINFORD-BRENT: I saw M. S. Dhoni in Boots at Birmingham train station the other day. He was in his India tracksuit so I was surprised he wasn't getting mobbed. He was in the same aisle that I was, so maybe he was buying exfoliating facial wash, too. He did give me a second look, but I don't know whether he recognized me or thought I was stalking him.

ALISON MITCHELL: Who's to say he wasn't stalking you, Ebony?

England v India, T20 International, Edgbaston, September 2014

Champagne Moments

England had just regained the Ashes after a bruising, controversial series.

BRIAN JOHNSTON: Illingworth is being chaired off by his team. It looks a bit precarious … and the police are there to stop someone coming to slap him on the back. Two small boys are being chased by policemen but it's definitely Illingworth's day. He's being chaired off and it looks like he might fall off at any moment.

Australia v England, Sydney, February 1971

• • •

The first streaker in English cricket, though John Arlott invented another term …

JOHN ARLOTT: So Woolmer 6, Knot 11, England 399 for 6. There's some signals going on to the dressing room. Woolmer is running in, lots of people are running out. Old is bringing Woolmer, what? A glass of water? Unusual … And a freaker! We've got a freaker down the wicket now. Not very shapely. And it's masculine. And I would think it's seen the last of its cricket for the day. The police are mustered, so are the cameramen, and Greg Chappell … No, he's had his load. He's being embraced by a blond policeman and this may be his last public appearance, but what a splendid one … and so warm! Many, of course, have done this on cold rugby grounds, but this chap has done it before 25,000 people on a day when he doesn't even feel cold. He's now being marched down, and the final exhibition, past at least 8000 people in the Mound Stand, some of whom perhaps have never quite seen anything like this before.

England v Australia, Lord's, August 1975

• • •

Geoff Boycott needed only one more century to become the first man to score 100 first-class hundreds, on his home ground in Leeds.

FRED TRUEMAN: ... I've just been sat outside and you can feel it ... There are people holding their hearts when he plays a shot. The one he hit in the air over there, there were two chaps by the side of me who nearly passed out.

CHRISTOPHER MARTIN JENKINS: Well, let's hope nobody does, because nobody would want to miss it ... Chappell turns, goes in again. Boycott, 96 not out. He bowls to him ... it's a half-volley ... he drives it down the ground and there it is! He's done it. He lifts both hands in the air. Geoff Boycott has got his 100th hundred. And the crowd cannot resist coming on to the pitch any longer ...

England v Australia, Headingley, August 1977

• • •

David Gower's Test debut.

JOHN ARLOTT: Now instead of Roope, Gower is coming in. Gower of Leicestershire, Kentish-born. The young left-hander who is England's cricketer of the moment. This splendid, stylish strokemaker, superb timer of the ball, and this couldn't have been better stage-managed than that he should come in at this moment. Wasim Bari has decided to put the pressure on him. Let's see to what extent ... two slips, two gullies for the left-handed Gower and to bowl at him, Liaqat Ali, left-arm fast-medium over the wicket. And Liaqat comes in and bowls to Gower ... and Gower turns and hits his first ball in Test cricket for four behind square leg. Ah, what a princely entry. He is a good player, this boy. Perhaps the one really class batsman in the side ... and he's hit his first ball in Test cricket for four, and if that doesn't make him feel better he's a very odd young man, as well as a brilliant one.

England v Pakistan, Edgbaston, June 1978

TEST MATCH
MASTERMIND

News had reached the TMS *box that a member of the*
public had appeared on BBC TV show Mastermind
and had chosen Geoffrey Boycott as his specialist subject.
During a break in play, Jonathan Agnew decided to test
the great man himself with the same questions ...

JONATHAN AGNEW: So, as promised, it's time for *Mastermind* … [*theme tune plays*]. Could I have your name?

GEOFF BOYCOTT: Geoffrey Boycott.

JA: Occupation?

GB (*laughs*): Retired.

JA: And your chosen specialist subject?

GB: Geoffrey Boycott.

JA: You have two minutes on your favourite chosen specialist subject, Geoffrey Boycott, and it's over to John Humphrys for the first question …

JOHN HUMPHRYS (*voice recorded*): In 1977 at which ground did Boycott reach his 100th first-class century, the first person to do so in a Test match?

GB: Headingley, Yorkshire.

JA: Correct … Your second question …

JH: What was the name of the Government office in Barnsley where Boycott worked as a clerical officer after he left school and before he became a professional cricketer?

GB: Ministry of Pensions and National Insurance in Barnsley, 9–11 Regent Street. I had to walk from the bus station up the hill.

JA: Correct … Third question.

JH: He twice had a batting average of over a hundred in an English first-class season. In 1971 and in which other year?

GB: 1979. Do you want the average?

JA: No need. Please confine your answers to the question. Correct. Question four …

JH: Who was sacked as Yorkshire captain at the end of the 1970 season, leading to Boycott being appointed to the position?

GB: Dennis Brian Close … probably one of the worst decisions Yorkshire ever made. I wanted him to stay, I really did. He was a fine captain.

JA: What, making you captain was the worst decision or …

GB (*laughs*): Both of them.

JA: Correct. On both counts. Question five.

JH: As a teenager Boycott played a handful of games for which football club's under-18s team?

GB: Leeds United. I once played with Billy Bremner in the Northern Intermediate Cup at Doncaster.

JA: Correct. I'm worried about this one … question six.

JH: Who was Chairman of Selectors when Boycott was dropped from the Test team for scoring 'too slowly' in his 246 not out in the first Test against India in 1967?

GB: Very easy … they should have spelled his name with an 'A'. His name is Insole. Douglas.

JA: Correct. To John Humphrys for question seven …

JH: In his match commentary for a Test played in January 2012, Boycott said that he would sell his three houses if England did not win. They eventually did lose. To which country?

GB (*laughs*): How could they not get 140 against Pakistan? Idiots.

JA: Correct. Was that the date?

GB: Yes. Then Rachel [his wife] rang up within minutes and she said, 'You can let them have your half, but they're not having mine!'

JA: You're doing well so far. You've got seven out of seven. Question eight.

JH: He lived with his mother in a terraced house in the former mining village of Fitzwilliam, south-east of Wakefield, until her death in 1978. What was the name of the street they lived on?

GB: Milton Terrace, number 45.

JA: Correct … Question nine …

JH: Boycott was famously out for a duck against the West Indies in Bridgetown in 1981 when he was bowled by the final ball of a rapid over from which bowler?

GB: Michael Holding, 'Whispering Death'.

JA: You're doing well, that's nine out of nine. Question ten …

JH: In August 2008, Boycott stated in his *Daily Telegraph* column that team huddles before play should stop. It's cosmetic, he said, and done for the cameras. 'It's like big girls before …' What?

GB:

Yes, I did say something like that … 'It's like big girls before netball' or something.

JA: You're struggling.

GB: I am struggling.

JA: Are you passing on that?

GB: Yes.

JA: A hockey match, Geoffrey.

GB: I knew it was something. I'd seen my daughter and her girls at school do it. I thought, 'This is ridiculous.'

JA: Right. And the final question …

JH: What is the name of the South African team that Boycott briefly played for in the 1971/2 season for whom he scored a century against Rhodesia?

GB: Northern Transvaal …

JA: Here's your last question, in fact, from John Humphrys …

JH: In December 1981 whose record of most runs in Test matches did he beat while he was playing in the third Test against India?

GB: Gary Sobers at Feroz Kotla, Delhi.

JA: You're correct. Those were all they had time for on the programme.

GB: And you've got some up your sleeve, haven't you?

JA: We have the reserve ones. So far you have eleven out of twelve. What was Geoff Boycott's highest score in Test cricket? These are the ones John Humphrys didn't have a chance to ask because time ran out.

GB: 246 not out at Headingley in 1967 …

JA: Correct. What grammar school did Boycott attend?

GB: Hemsworth Grammar School.

JA: Correct. Who opened the batting with Geoff Boycott in his debut test against Australia in 1964?

GB: Good question that … a lot don't get it. Freddie Titmus.

JA: Yes … Did you run him out?

GB: Nearly! Actually it was very interesting. We went for a run and did you know he was deaf in one ear? He can't hear, Freddie. He really has no idea. You called for a run and it was like a negotiation. He's putting his hand to his ear to see if he can hear anything. And he set off and Neil Hawke, who bowled the ball, ran to pick up the ball on the on side, knocked him over. It knocked him flat … out, he was. Neil Hawke was a former Australian Rules player, which you have to be physically fit for. And he threw the ball in to Wally Grout and Wally Grout got the ball above the stumps … Titmus is still flat … and he just threw the ball back. Great sportsman.

JA: How many of Boycott's 108 Test matches did England lose? Twenty? Forty? Or sixty?

GB (*repeats question*): ... Well, it has to be 20.

JA: Correct.

GB: Can't be 40 because, listen – they never lost a Test match where I made a hundred. They were either won or drawn. Never in 22 hundreds.

JA: In his childhood, Geoff Boycott had two pet rabbits. What were their names?

GB: Oh, my God, I can't remember them! One was a great big Belgian silver something ... silver blue ...

JA: Like a gorilla!

GB: Oh no, he was a lovely big thing. I can't remember that. Are you making this up?

JA: No, it's one of the questions.

GB: I can't remember the rabbit's name!

JA: You had two of them. Well, you had to drop a question there … you passed. The problem is we don't know the answer either … What was Boycott's strike rate in One-Day Internationals? Was it: 93.36. Or, was it lower than Jonathan Agnew's at 53.36?

GB: Yes, it was lower than yours. That little wizard was in New York when he sent that question, wasn't he? That little wizard [*Boycott was referring to Daniel Radcliffe, the actor who played Harry Potter*].

JA: Geoffrey Boycott was involved in 20 run-outs in Test cricket. But how many involved himself and how many involved his partner?

GB: Most of them didn't run fast enough, Jonathan …

JA: Just answer the question.

GB: I can't … you made that up.

JA: Only seven, were you. You ran out 13 of your partners.

GB: No! Twelve of them didn't run fast enough …

JA: Which partner did you run out most? Edrich, Randall or Gooch.

GB: Edrich.

JA: Yes, poor old John.

GB:

Well, he was small! He took small steps. He didn't run fast.

JA: Edrich three times, Randall twice, Gooch twice.

JA: What vegetable did your mother use as a bat?

GB (*laughter*): Rhubarb.

JA: Which episode of *CSI* did Geoff Boycott go and watch when he put down the phone in a BBC interview?

GB: Not telling you. *Miami, Las Vegas* … I like 'em all.

JA: This an either/or, A or B, multiple choice question. What sort of pitch did Geoff Boycott prefer to bat on? Covered or uncovered?

GB: Uncovered.

JA: Well done, Geoffrey. Our contestant [on *Mastermind*] got eight. Geoffrey did rather better than that. But, hey, it's your specialist subject, isn't it?

GB: Shut up.

The next day's play, and the names of his two rabbits still eluded Boycott.

GB: … I definitely didn't know the name of my two rabbits.

JA: Any news on that?

GB: That really did stump me. I'm going to ring my brother.

JA: He'll know.

GB: Yeah. I were trying to think about it all last night. I was watching the football and I'm thinking about two rabbits!

JA: They sounded like nice rabbits.

GB: Lovely Belgian, bluey grey he was … I can picture it! Aaah!

JA: Flopsy?

GB: No! Not daft names like that!

JA: Hobbs? Sutcliffe?

The next day Boycott took the chance to turn the tables on a surprised Aggers …

JONATHAN AGNEW: Oh, Geoffrey …

GEOFF BOYCOTT: Yes! Can I have your name, please?

JA: Jonathan Agnew.

GB: What's your occupation? If you've got one …

JA: Part-time commentator …

GB: Yeah … and your specialist subject?

JA: I don't know. You tell me.

GB: Jonathan Agnew. It won't be very long …

JA: Geoffrey, I can't believe you're doing this …

GB: Right. Who took more wickets in Test cricket? Jonathan Agnew or Geoff Boycott?

JA: Geoff Boycott.

GB: Aha! One for Geoffrey. Who was Jonathan Agnew's first Test match wicket?

JA: Gordon Greenidge.

GB: Hmmm. You didn't get many, did you? How many runs did Jonathan Agnew score in his first Test?

JA: The whole match? I don't know. Four?

GB: No. Five and two. Not many was it?

JA: Who's researched all these?

GB: In which year was Jonathan Agnew named one of *Wisden*'s Cricketers of the Year? You're kidding me. Did they really give you that?

JA: 1988. Eighty-seven …

GB: Who were the idiots on the board then? Yeah, you're dead right. Jonathan Agnew had a first cousin who played Test cricket. Who was that?

JA: Mary Duggan.

GB: You're right. England women's team. '48 to '63.

JA: She was captain.

GB: When Jonathan Agnew left school in 1978 he had two A levels … that's one more than I would give him. In what subjects?

JA: I don't think I did, I think I only had one … German.

GB: Yeah.

JA: And English?

GB: Wow, you're dead right.

JA: But they weren't proper passes. I think they were a D and an E.

GB: Well, it says that you got them anyhow. With which fellow England cricketer did Jonathan Agnew save the life of a woman on England's tour of India in 1984?

JA: Bruce French.

GB: Correct.

JA: Fisherman's Cove outside Madras. We agreed to keep it quiet. Not to tell any of the press, and French went and told the press.

GB: In 1978 Ray Illingworth in *The Times* was quoted as saying Jonathan Agnew was the second fastest bowler in the country. But who did he say was the fastest?

JA: At the time?

GB: Well, I've known Raymond, ooh …

JA: He's a great judge, a very canny judge …

GB: … must be 40-odd years and I've never known him lie 'til now. Saying you were the second fastest in the country …

JA: So the other one wasn't faster than me then?

GB: He was. But he's lying about you.

JA: Who was the other one then?

GB: You've failed. Bob Willis. Which England captain did Jonathan Agnew strike in the face with a ball in the nets when invited to bowl at the England tourists on tour of Australia in 1978/9?

JA: You've heard of this one. I've never seen a panic like it because they thought you might have to captain the side instead. Mike Brearley, and I was very unpopular.

GB: All them brains, he went to Cambridge, and he went to the nets when it were wet and you hit him on the top of the head. I said, 'Don't go in there, you'll get hit.'

JA: Hit him in the eye … a black eye came up.

GB: … Although commonly known as Aggers, which United States Vice-President is Jonathan nicknamed after ?

JA: Yeah, Spiro. I'm called that by two people. Ian Botham and Ian Chappell, both of whom hate each other. It's the one thing they have in common.

GB: Against which county did Jonathan make a one-match comeback for Leicestershire? Two years after retirement …

JA: Essex.

GB: Yeah, I thought you'd remember that …

JA: Semi-final …

GB: In 2005 what broadcast from Jonathan was voted the greatest sporting commentary of all time?

JA: Well, that'll be the 'legover', but don't vote for it again. It wasn't great commentary, it was, in your words [*puts on Yorkshire accent*] 'It were a cock-up, Geoffrey'.

GB: I've heard it. It was funny. Now, this was one of my favourites …

JA: We're not on to pet rabbits, are we?

GB: No. How many runs did Sidath Wettimuny score in the first innings of Jonathan Agnew's second Test match at Lord's?

JA: It was a lot.

GB: Yeah, I bet you enjoyed bowling at him.

JA: I'm going for 182.

GB: 190 [*giggles*].

JA: Was it?

GB: Yeah, I bet it didn't swing much there, Jonathan.

JA: There was a very short boundary to be fair, Geoffrey, on one side …

GB: Should've bowled at the other end …

JA: … down to the Tavern. I did. I bowled every end.

GB: What were Jonathan's match figures at Lord's v Sri Lanka in 1984?

JA (*pauses*): 2 for 200?

GB: 2 for plenty. 2 for 77, 2 for 177 or 2 for 277.

JA: I think 177.

GB: Yeah, that's about right. What was the reaction of Bay 13 when Jonathan fielded on the boundary at the MCG Melbourne in his final One-Day International in 1985?

JA: … There were a few reactions. There was the offer of drinking something that was supposed to be beer and definitely wasn't.

GB: Something better than that …

JA: There was a certain amount of flashing going on.

GB: That was the one! How can you get flashed on the boundary?

JA: … It was male flashing and it wasn't very pretty.

GB: You scored 12 points.

JA: That better than you?

GB: No.

India v England, Mumbai, November 2012

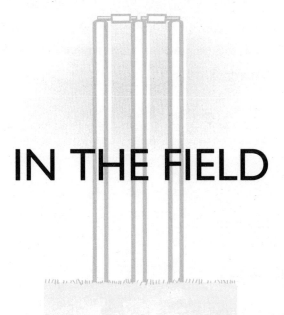

IN THE FIELD

JOHN ARLOTT: Now, in comes Khan and bowls to him [Denis Compton] and he cracks that to back down to mid-off, but mid-off is – I was going to say respectfully deep … mid-off's position is a women and children first position. They're obviously about to take to the boats.

England v Pakistan, Trent Bridge, July 1954

• • •

JOHN ARLOTT: Fielders scattering like missionaries to far places.

Date unknown

• • •

JOHN ARLOTT: 77 they [New Zealand] now want with five wickets to fall, and Arnold bowls to Wadsworth … and he edges it and he's magnificently caught! He is quite splendidly caught by Roope going far, far to his right at second slip, and let me say there are not more than three or four people in

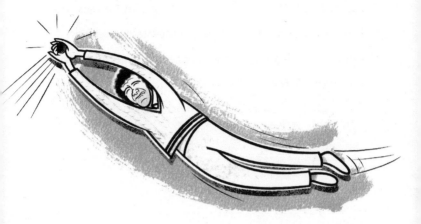

English cricket today who would have caught that.
It must have been at least six feet wide of his right
foot as he stood at second slip and he got across,
took it two-handed. Bill Frindall reminds me that
he's a goalkeeper. He took it two-handed, goalkeeper
fashion, away wide to his right, and Wadsworth is
short of the 50 that would have come if that had
been missed. Caught Roope, bowled Arnold, 46. 402
for 6 – and the game is now back in the hazard, as
the tennis players say.

England v New Zealand, Trent Bridge, June 1973

• • •

JOHN ARLOTT: Massie bowls, Illingworth edges, and he's caught by Stackpole at second slip. He [Stackpole] was one of those who had none of the booty until then.

England v Australia, Lord's, June 1972

• • •

BRIAN JOHNSTON: Up comes Holder now, bowls this one outside the off stump, and it's steered away on the off side. Nice bit of fielding by Julian there – there might be overthrows here, and there are. They've taken one and they're taking a second one. So three runs to Knott from a ball he steered from outside the off stump – and there's going to be more! There's going to be four overthrows added to that. So Knott has got seven. They're trying to work out which end they've got to go to …

BILL FRINDALL: [Umpire] Spencer signalled six.

BJ: Spencer signalled six, which is extraordinary. But they've got to work out which end to go to.

Knott should be at the other end if they ran seven. Dear chap, that's right, you go up there. They're arguing like mad and they're both coming to the same end, but it must be right for Knott to go to the other end.

BF (*incredulous*): It's one plus two plus four …

BJ: Both the umpires are consulting now. This is the best muddle – it's marvellous. Oh, it's lovely. Knott doesn't know which end to come to. I can tell him, he should be at the other end and they're leaving him at this end. [Umpire] Constant is talking to Knott … oh and 'one short' was called. That doesn't make a difference to which end they go … Knott's going down the other end now and Spencer's talking to Greig. This is absolutely splendid, isn't it? Both the umpires are consulting, the two batsmen are there, everyone is in a state of flummox. Lloyd is getting in on the act. But … if it's seven runs, then Knott must be at the other end.

BF: Even if it's six and one short.

BJ: We're trying to work out if it is one short but all these signals … now he's signalling byes! Well, that can't be right … two short is he signalling? …

BF: He's signalling five plus two … I think he's signalling seven.

BJ: Well, Knott has gone to 41 on the board so they've given him nine, haven't they? No, he was 34. That's right, they've given him seven. That was absolutely splendid. One of the best things I've seen in Test cricket.

England v West Indies, Headingley, July 1976

• • •

JOHN ARLOTT: The anguish on his [umpire Dickie Bird's] countenance is something the great actors of the past would have given anything [for]. Imagine [Sir Henry] Irving, if he could have registered suffering as Dick does when he puts his boot in a quarter of an inch of water, and hoists his trousers to his calves, to pretend he's being splashed. This is one of the great dramatic presentations of all time.

England v Australia, Lord's, August 1980

• • •

BRIAN JOHNSTON: In comes Sobers, well-pitched up, and driven hard into the ground there and fielded by Sobers himself. No-ball is called by Arthur Fagg, pointing majestically towards Father Time …

Date unknown

• • •

BRIAN JOHNSTON: What sort of duties does the twelfth man carry out, Fred?

FRED TRUEMAN: Not something I had any experience of, Brian.

Date unknown

• • •

I reckon my mum could have caught that in her pinny!

GEOFF BOYCOTT (*on a dropped catch*)

• • •

GEOFF BOYCOTT (*on another dropped catch*):
He could have caught that between the cheeks of
his backside.

Date unknown

• • •

HENRY BLOFELD: There's a throw at the stumps by Ahmed. It's gone for four overthrows so five runs, buzzers, indeed! Buzzers like mad … We always used to call it buzzers when I played cricket at school. When I've said it before people have looked at me as if I was an absolute lunatic, which might be so, but I've always called them buzzers.

Date unknown

• • •

Substitute Gary Pratt was fielding for England, and about to become an unlikely hero …

HENRY BLOFELD: Here comes Andrew Flintoff, in now to Ponting. He bowls and Ponting comes forward, plays it out on the off side and they go for a quick single, Pratt … hits them! That's probably run out! A marvellous piece of fielding by Gary Pratt and umpire Aleem Dar signals for the third umpire. The England players think they've got him … they're all round Pratt, congratulating him. Well, it was a marvellous piece of fielding … Yes, he's out, he's clearly out, and that really is the wicket England most wanted … the substitute Gary Pratt has now been lifted up, chair-lifted, by his fellows.

England v Australia, Trent Bridge, August 2005

• • •

JONATHAN AGNEW: I saw him [Alastair Cook] muttering something there that he wouldn't have muttered in the stalls of St Paul's when he was a choirboy.

England v India, Champions Trophy Final, Edgbaston, June 2013

Champagne Moments

CHRISTOPHER MARTIN JENKINS: Graham Gooch, bowled Prabhakar 333. Almost the world stopped for a second in amazement, and then the crowd erupted in congratulations for Prabhakar and still greater congratulations for the England captain, Graham Gooch of Essex, who has succumbed at what some people might think is an unlucky score of 333. He and the crowd who saw it will never forget this innings. Off comes his white helmet, up comes his weighty blade, risen to the crowd …

FAROKH ENGINEER: Lovely to see the whole England team clapping him all the way to the pavilion. The non-striker Robin Smith, his bat down, his gloves off, clapping him. I think even [umpire] Dickie Bird had a few claps and it's fantastic – what a superb innings and the proverbial Nelson has done it again, 333.

CMJ: Done it again? When did you last see it done?

● ● ●

Later in the match, India needed 24 to avoid the follow-on with their last pair together, Hirwani and the great Kapil Dev.

CHRISTOPHER MARTIN JENKINS: There's a forward short leg as the only close fielder and a man at fine leg about 15 yards in from the fence. There are four men out towards the leg-side boundary, two on the off side and a forward short leg. Up comes Hemmings. He bowls – and this is a big hit. It has gone right over the sightscreen for a six! And a massive stroke it was. It hit the little bit of tarpaulin that separates the two new stands, and it would have

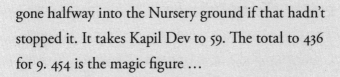

gone halfway into the Nursery ground if that hadn't stopped it. It takes Kapil Dev to 59. The total to 436 for 9. 454 is the magic figure ...

Hemmings bowls, down the pitch he comes, tries it again, it's going to be another six! Over long on, miles over long on. It was about nine again, not six.

TREVOR BAILEY: Lovely shot. He doesn't half hit the ball. It's the high backlift. And now I reckon he wants a single.

CMJ: 65 to him – what a marvellous bit of batting by Kapil Dev. Hemmings quite rightly giving him the bait. He comes in now and that's a bit flatter. He goes for the hit again. He could be caught ... no, it's another six! Three in a row! That was lower and even harder off a ball that was not tossed up. Eighteen off three balls.

BILL FRINDALL: That's equalled the world record for three successive sixes, the most ever hit. Sylvester Clarke and Walter Hammond – but not in the same match.

CMJ: This has been one of the best morning's cricket I have ever seen, I think. 448 for 9. Kapil Dev 71 not out. And now India, from being absolutely at the Gates of Doom so to speak, if you consider the follow-on in cricketing terms potential doom anyway, now they are at the Gates of Paradise, because they need only six more – and that can be done in one shot.

TB: It's a very difficult one. I can't read Kapil Dev's mind.

CMJ: One more ball in the over.

TB: My own feeling is go for the single now. But I think he might go for another biggie.

CMJ: You didn't often go for four sixes in a row, Trevor. Well, here's the last ball of the over. Hemmings bowls it. Kapil Dev is going for the big hit. It's going to do it, is it? He's done it! He's saved the follow-on. He's broken a world record. He shakes his fist to the Indian dressing room and if that isn't

one of the most remarkable things you've ever seen in cricket, I don't know what is. Four sixes in a row, just when England seemed to have it all sewn up. Fantastic batting.

TB: I'm speechless. I've never seen that happen before. I don't think I shall ever see it happen again.

CMJ: He's smiling, as well he might.

BF: He's not only beaten the record for the most sixes off consecutive balls, he's equalled the record for the most runs in a six-ball over. That's the fourth instance of 24.

TB: And in that situation!

CMJ: Incredible. Well, 454 for 9, Fraser bowls to Hirwani. It keeps low. He's lbw! Well, what an extraordinary game is cricket and what a wonderful game this has been.

England v India, Lord's, July 1990

• • •

CHRISTOPHER MARTIN JENKINS: He's 98 not out and Fraser bowls to him. He drives it through mid-off and this is Sachin Tendulkar's first Test hundred, driven up towards the mid-off boundary. Lewis in pursuit, but they'll get three runs for it. And this 17-year-old has become the second youngest Test centurion in cricket history. What a wonderful performance. He takes off his helmet and politely waves his bat to the crowd at Old Trafford who stand to a man, woman and child to congratulate him. A heroic performance – really the stuff of which schoolboy novels were made.

England v India, Old Trafford, August 1990

SLIPS, GAGS
AND GAFFES

That's Harvey at leg slip there, with his legs wide apart ... waiting for a tickle.

BRIAN JOHNSTON

England v Australia, Headingley, July 1961

• • •

BRIAN JOHNSTON: It's going to be Snow to the crouching Henry Horton who looks like he's shitting, er, sitting on a shooting stick, without the shooting stick.

Sussex v Hampshire, Gillette Cup quarter-final, Hove, June 1967

• • •

BRIAN JOHNSTON (*Glenn Turner had been hit in the box by the fifth ball of the over*): It looks as if he's going to try and continue, though he still looks very shaken and pale. Very plucky of him. Yes, he's definitely going to have a try. One ball left …

England v New Zealand, 1969

• • •

BRIAN JOHNSTON: Do you know of any bowling mums in this country?

TREVOR BAILEY: Can't think of any.

BJ: What about Penny Cowdrey? Didn't you hear about her performance against her son's school at Broadstairs last week?

TB: No.

BJ: Really!? I'm surprised you didn't hear about it. I'm told her swingers were absolutely unplayable.

Date unknown

• • •

BRIAN JOHNSTON: You've come over at a very appropriate time. Ray Illingworth has just relieved himself at the Pavilion End.

Date unknown

• • •

BRIAN JOHNSTON: Goodbye from Southampton and now over to Edgbaston for some more balls from Rex Alston.

Date unknown

. . .

Yorkshire 232 all out. Hutton ill. No, I'm sorry – Hutton 111.

JOHN SNAGGE
Yorkshire v Leicestershire, Headingley, May 1946

. . .

BRIAN JOHNSTON: Bill [Frindall] needs a small ruler. How about the Sultan of Brunei? I hear he is only four foot ten.

Date unknown

• • •

JOHN ARLOTT: Bill Frindall has done a bit of mental arithmetic with a calculator.

Date unknown

• • •

Christopher Martin Jenkins was renowned for being disorganized and tardy. Occasionally he could even forget where he was …

BRIAN JOHNSTON: What an occasion here for Trent Bridge … This is the 150th anniversary … Saturday was the exact day 150 years ago when play first took place at Trent Bridge in 1838 … Christopher Martin Jenkins will be starting the commentary … good morning to you, Jenkers.

CMJ: Good morning to you, Brian. Good morning to everybody. Lovely it is to be back at Old Trafford … [*laughter*] Lovely it is to be back at Trent Bridge in a special year …

England v West Indies, Trent Bridge, June 1988

• • •

BRIAN JOHNSTON: Meanwhile, Botham had been joined by Lewis, and Botham in the end out in the most extraordinary way.

JONATHAN AGNEW: The tragic thing about it, he knew exactly what was going to happen and he tried to step over the stumps and just flicked a bail with his right leg.

BJ: To be honest he tried to do the splits over and unfortunately the inner part of his thigh must have just removed the bails.

JA: Yes, he just didn't quite get his leg over.

BJ: Anyhow, he did very well indeed, batting 131 minutes, and hit three fours, and then we had Lewis playing extremely well for his 47 not out …

JA: [*laughs*]

BJ: Aggers, do stop it … And he was joined by DeFreitas, who was in for 40 minutes, a useful little partnership there, they put on 35 in 40 minutes and then he was caught by Dujon off Walsh. Lawrence, always entertaining, batted for 35 … 35 minutes, hit a four … over the wicketkeeper's … Aggers, for goodness' sake, stop it … [*laughs uncontrollably*].

JA: Yes … Lawrence [*laughs uncontrollably*].

England v West Indies, The Oval, August 1991

• • •

Trevor Bailey's nickname was the Boil ...

I'm joined by the Balls, er, the Boil ...

BRIAN JOHNSTON

...

JONATHAN AGNEW: 'The cranial capacity of a skull can provide a reasonable estimate of the size of an animal's brain.' So there we are – Humpty Dumpty was quite clever, I think that means ... Humpty Dumpty bowls ... or Warne bowls [*laughs*]. Don't believe I said that ... I'm hoping the tape recorders in the van weren't recording for that particular moment. Oh, yes they were ... I've got a feeling that

moment will come back to haunt me at some stage.
Oh dear.

DAVID LLOYD: That really could be a champagne
moment. 'Humpty Dumpty comes in to bowl …'

England v Australia, 1993

• • •

CHRISTOPHER MARTIN JENKINS: Two slips, third man, [*hic*]… deep gully, cover, mid-off, mid-on, square leg and long leg the field [*hic*]. Excuse me, I have got hiccups for some reason. That's fielded at cover by Ramprakash. I'll try to time my hiccups so it's not when I'm talking …

TREVOR BAILEY: Now if we pushed our scorer out through the window and he was disappearing, you'd have a shock then …

BILL FRINDALL: I haven't got hiccups!

TB: But that would shock him!

CMJ: It would be really rather amusing.

England v Australia, 1993

• • •

JONATHAN AGNEW: [*coughs*] Excuse me [*voice is husky*] ... next ball, oh [*coughs*] my throat's gone ... Peter Baxter with a drink, thank you ...

GRAEME FOWLER: It's the shock of remembering one of your Test wickets which finally got to you ...

JA (*voice back to normal*): Must be one of those thunderflies which have been flying around the past few days, and went in the wrong way.

GF: Plenty of room to get in, though, wasn't there?

Date unknown

• • •

BRIAN JOHNSTON: 104 for 2, taken the lead up to ... one hundred and ninety ... one.

FRED TRUEMAN: Are you sure?

BJ: Yes. More or less. 87 add 4, 191.

FT: Well done. I mean, how much money did they spend on your education to get you to that height, to add 87 to 4?

BJ: I don't use computers or anything.

FT: Neither do I.

BJ: The Bearded Wonder does. You ask him to add 37 to 38 and he won't be able to without putting his fingers down on those things. I can tell you straight away that it's 77.

BILL FRINDALL: It's 75.

BJ: Well, it's very near …

Date unknown

DON MOSEY: So, as the umpires, who are Dickie Bird and Barrie Meyer, come to the middle and that massive erection at the City end of the ground comes into view, I will leave Brian Johnston to describe that and other matters to you …

England v West Indies, 1988

• • •

CHRISTOPHER MARTIN JENKINS: This time Vettori lets it go outside the off stump, good length, inviting him to fish but Vettori stays on the bank and keeps his rod down, so to speak … [*starts to laugh*]. I don't know if he's a fisherman [*giggles …*] [*regaining composure*] 208 for 6 as Broad from the Pavilion End comes in again [*laughter in the background*] … a lot of cricketers are fishermen … he bowls …

England v New Zealand, Lord's, May 2008

• • •

JONATHAN AGNEW: Just a warning for those of you who are coming out, and I know many of you are coming to Calcutta for the third Test match. They are taking sun cream off you as you come into the gate, which is not very funny actually in this part of the world. So if you can try and plot something deviously under your duvet, some means of bringing it in, because you do need it. Disguise it about your person or something. I don't think they'll necessarily give you an intimate search, and I don't mean that intimate, but I think if you were cunning, you could probably, er, anyway I making a mess of it here … that's outside the off stump and Pietersen flashes at it and it's taken by Dhoni.

VIC MARKS: Thank goodness Ojha came up to bowl again.

India v England, Mumbai, November 2012

• • •

VIC MARKS: By and large he's done a pretty good job …

JONATHAN AGNEW: Oh my word! I'm sorry … something hideous has flown in … and it's enormous … It's a bird. Help. Hang on … What sort of bird?

VM: Well, I don't know what sort of bird …

JA: Whoa!

VM: … but it's gone. It's flown out of the window.

JA: I haven't ducked like that since Sylvester Clarke bowled me a bouncer.

VM: The trouble is there was no short leg for you to aim at really.

JA: Phew …

VM:

Well, you were very, very brave. Braver than your fellow commentator, I think.

...

HENRY BLOFELD: In the rear, the small diminutive figure of Shoaib Mohammad, who can't be much taller than he is.

Date unknown

• • •

After watching Kevin Pietersen replace the grip on his bat, Aggers had been discussing the difficulties of applying a new grip.

JONATHAN AGNEW: Michael Vaughan is beside me. It's not easy putting a rubber on, is it?

MICHAEL VAUGHAN: No, it's not. I was never very good at that. [*Laughter*]

JA: You know what I meant.

MV: Shall we move on?

England v Sri Lanka, Lord's, June 2011

Champagne Moments

A match that needs no introduction ...

HENRY BLOFELD: 58 for 3, Australia needing 130 to win. They want 72 more runs and this game is by no means over. A tight attacking field, and here is Willis again, bowling for his life, bowls now to Yallop, and ... he is out! He is caught at forward short leg – he is caught by Gatting. It lifted on him, he played it, could not keep it down, Gatting came forward, got both hands to it, threw it in the air and Australia go to lunch at 58 for 4. Yallop caught Gatting bowled Willis for 0. Well, Fred, what an over!

FRED TRUEMAN: What an over, what a transformation!

Later that day …

HENRY BLOFELD: Oh dear, oh dear, pulse rates … I wonder how many heart attacks around the country? People watching this on television, listening to it over the radio …

TREVOR BAILEY: Most of the Australian side inside the dressing room cannot watch.

HB: Could you watch? Were you good at watching?

TB: No. Not watching. Playing, yes …

HB: Well, it's Willis now, Willis to Bright. Bright is 19, Australia 111 for 9, 19 short of victory. Here is Willis, in, bowls to Bright … Bright bowled! The middle stump is out of the ground! England have won! They have won by 18 runs! Willis runs around

punching the air, the boys invade the ground and
the players run helter-skelter for the pavilion. Well,
what a finish. Bright bowled Willis for 19, Willis has
taken 8 for 43 – the best ever by an English bowler
here at Headingley against Australia, a phenomenal
performance by Bob Willis and Australia all out for
111. England have won by 18 runs.

England v Australia, Headingley, July 1981

• • •

The final was truly a David and Goliath affair …

CHRISTOPHER MARTIN JENKINS: In comes
Amaranth again … he's out! Lbw! He pulled across
the line, Holding, and India have caused one of the
greatest upsets in the history of all sport. They have
won the third Prudential World Cup, beating the hot
favourites, the 1-4 on favourites, the West Indies.

India v West Indies, World Cup final, Lord's, June 1983

A LISTENER WRITES …

Letters and emails from listeners around the world on a variety of subjects have always been the subject of discussion, and much amusement, in the TMS *box.*

BRIAN JOHNSTON: Fred, you'd be interested, a chap called David Taylor from Sunderland has sent me the definition of the word 'mosey'. Which I think knowing the Alderman [*Johnners' nickname for fellow commentator Don Mosey*] you'd be interested to hear.

FRED TRUEMAN: Yes, I would.

BJ: 'The word is not in the dictionary but is in frequent use in the Midland counties to express the condition of a turnip when the interior has become dry and fibrous, or of an apple when it has become withered and juiceless. It is equivalent to the term woolly, which is used in a similar sense in the southern counties.' Well, the Alderman now knows why he was called Mosey ... but there we are. I don't know about a turnip, but dry and fibrous ...

FT: Withered and juiceless.

BJ: No, you can't say that of the Alderman. It's unfair. I take it all back. But thanks for sending it to us all the same.

Date unknown

• • •

JONATHAN AGNEW: ... he's been inspired to write after watching the 'Australian moustache on legs' bowl with such savagery at Old Trafford – he's talking about Merv Hughes, of course. So then Keith comes up with his own Moustache Eleven. Not a bad team, actually. How about this: we've got Graham Gooch, Gordon Greenidge, Javed Miandad, Greg Chappell, Clive Lloyd, the captain, he had quite a big one, didn't he? Ian Botham, Rodney Marsh, Sir Richard Hadlee [*laughter from box, including Johnners' distinctive wheezy laugh*], Dennis Lillee, Merv Hughes and [*pause*] Mushtaq Ahmed. 273 for 1 [*laughs*].

FRED TRUEMAN: Is that team bowling?

JA: I don't know what they're doing. All sorts of ridiculous laughter from the background. Tufnell comes and bowls now to Boon, who goes back and across and plays the ball back along the pitch, Smith fields from silly point.

FT: Oh, I see. Are they having a go at you, Jonathan? Do you think? It will be inspired no doubt by that wonderful schoolboy Brian Johnston.

JA: It always is …

England v Australia, 1993

• • •

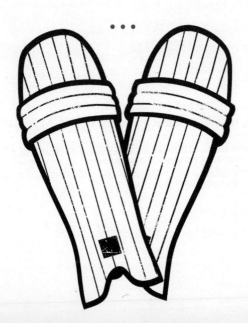

BRIAN JOHNSTON: I got this letter about whether they can be lbw with the pitching outside leg stump ... very interesting letter. I'm not quite sure who it's from [*laughter*] ... no, it's a perfectly good letter, addressed to me from The Laurels, Diss, in Norfolk. Thanks very much, Mr Biggun, for writing that one ... [*laughte*r].

England v Australia, 1993

• • •

JONATHAN AGNEW: Do you want a quickie before the umpires come out? 'Can you explain why, in a game of cricket, an appeals procedure is justifiable?' This comes from [*laughs*]... Berkshire ... [*Aggers and Johnners laugh*].

BRIAN JOHNSTON: It's not the Prime Minister William Pitt, but this is William H. Tit. He says can you ... [*unable to speak with laughter*].

Date unknown

• • •

BRIAN JOHNSTON: I have a nice letter from a chap named Gary Cassin who relates a good story when his team had two people, one was a young bowler named Roy Anscough and the father was the umpire and he was called Roland Anscough ... and they had a match and the whole thing depended on the last ball and there was this young boy Roy bowling, and he ran up to bowl and hit the batsman on the pad and his father, the umpire, appealed, and the boy gave it out and they all went off the field. Now, it's the first time I've known of an umpire appealing and the bowler giving it out. Have you ever heard that one, Fred?

FRED TRUEMAN: Not heard that one, no. It could only be sent to you, that one.

BJ: They all went off laughing. I don't think they'd do that in a Test match.

Date unknown

• • •

FRED TRUEMAN: It is a fax transmission from James Davies, Manipulative and Sports Physiotherapist of Essex County Cricket Club ...

JONATHAN AGNEW: It's Jim ...

FT: Well, I'll talk about fast bowling, Mr Davies, and I will not be faxing you about physiotherapy.

JA: Illott comes in and bowls to Mark Waugh who flicks the ball through midwicket, a misfield by Robin Smith, the ball has run away towards the boundary. It shouldn't get there, it's Peter Such now giving rather painful chase, he reaches the ball

now, the Waughs have run three, the throw is on its
way and that's all they'll have from a nicely timed
stroke. Robin Smith still crouching at midwicket still
wondering quite how the ball got through his hands.
139 for 4 ...

FT: England could do with a wicket ... But no,
thank you, James, for your fax, of course. He says:
'I've been listening to your radio commentary this
morning and I would like to correct your solid belief
that a fast bowler ...

JA: Illott bowls short to Steve Waugh who runs the
ball down to the gully ...

FT: James says, 'I would like to correct your solid
belief that a fast bowler does not have to get side-on
to deliver an outswinging delivery.' Well, I mean, I
say he *does* have to get sideways on to be able to swing
the ball and that the left elbow should be pointing
somewhere towards fine leg and the left shoulder
posting down the wicket towards the batsman ...

JA: Illott comes in over the wicket and bowls short again to Steve Waugh who gets right behind the ball and plays it out on the off side. Atherton strolls in and fields and there's no run …

FT: I have constantly said that I don't think he can get sideways on because the lad had an operation, and I've been saying that, haven't I? And he says, 'The reason why Mark Illott's right foot is where it is, and his chest is front-on, is the fundamental reason why he has made a successful return to top-class bowling following a spinal stress fracture and a screw fusion.' Well, I've been on about this operation and why he can't get sideways …

JA: Illott bowls again and that's on middle and off and Steve Waugh pushes it to Atherton in the covers and once again there's no run.

FT: He says, 'I spent many hours rehabilitating this potent left-arm swing bowler in the hope of eliminating the cause factors of the back pain which irresponsible and short-sightedness from commentators such as yourself seem intent on introducing. When will you listen and learn and read the wealth of information available and thereby reduce the incidence of low back pain in potential fast bowlers?'

JA: Right, it's Illott now who bowls a bouncer to Steve Waugh, ducks underneath it and allows the ball to pass through to Alec Stewart. Illott following through a long way there, and having a little glare in Steve Waugh's direction. It's the end of the over. 139 for 4. Steve Waugh has 15 and Mark Waugh has 76.

FT: He says, [*incredulous voice*] 'I would only be too grateful to help you.' Well, without blowing my own trumpet, James Davies, as one of the most successful fast bowlers of all time, I don't think you can give me much advice on how to bowl and swing the ball. 'To illustrate my point, a left-arm swing bowler can remain very front-on in order to move the ball [*even more incredulous voice*] in the air, as demonstrated by Bruce Reid's annihilation of England in 1990/91. He, in fact, manipulates the angle of the wrist.' Well, I

suggest you give up physiotherapy and start teaching people how to bowl fast. I'll stop talking about it.

JA: Well, let's watch Emburey come in and bowl short to Mark Waugh, he steers the ball firmly into the covers off the back foot. It's fielded by Mike Atherton at extra cover ...

FT: What do you make of it?

JA: Unfortunately it's not addressed to me, Fred [*laughter*]. Emburey comes and bowls to Mark Waugh, who flicks that firmly to midwicket and it's fielded by Matthew Maynard, who's got the sunglasses on now ...

FT:

I think I might know a little bit about fast bowling ...

England v Australia, Edgbaston, August 1993

• • •

CHRISTOPHER MARTIN JENKINS: I don't know
if I should read out this email from Anne-Marie
Briggs. But I'm going to. 'It was great to listen to
the lunchtime item about past commentators and it
brought back a lot of memories. I can't understand
how most of those who are still commentating only
sounded a bit younger on the old recordings, whereas
CMJ not only sounded a lot older, but also sounded
like the love child of Terry Thomas and a Dalek.'
She wants me to say exterminate during the course
of my commentary. I might oblige you, Anne-Marie,
in just a moment ... Here comes Bravo trying to
exterminate Collingwood. He plays it back up the
pitch. [*Dalek voice*] 'Exterminate!' Will that do it for
you? That's the last time I'll do it, I assure you. And
I am, in fact, getting younger.

England v West Indies, 2007

England were striving for the last wickets to win on the fourth day and reclaim the Ashes. As always, across the world, in weird and wonderful places, men and women stopped to listen to TMS.

CHRISTOPHER MARTIN JENKINS: Tuffers, England had better win this today to help out Dave who has emailed the programme to say: 'I'm listening by satellite phone with a confused German, a disinterested Austrian and, best of all, a despondent Australian at Everest Base Camp. Watching the sun go down after a day's acclimatization before beginning a four-man ascent of Everest tomorrow. So need England to wrap it up today!'

We've also had an email from Ewan and Jose, two seal and penguin scientists from the British Antarctic Survey who are listening on the Bird Island Research Station on South Georgia on the icy Southern Ocean. They want to thank *TMS* for bringing 'a little taste of summer in the depths of our winter'.

And Peter Edgerton emailed us to say he was 'listening from the rock face of Gimmer Crag high above the Langdale Valley. I have been able to update other parties from time to time on the progress of the game!'

These emails prompted more. Later in the day ...

CMJ: We've had a text from one listener tuning to *TMS* via his mobile phone on a beach in Ghana. His message is that his wife had forgotten to pack a phone charger and he is desperately searching for a listener who would just happen to be also on the same beach and could help.

Later ...

CMJ: Tuffers – you are not going to believe what has happened – Josh Grainger has contacted the programme to say: 'Hello, I heard the email you've just read out, and I have got two spare phone chargers, I'm in Halloway Beach in Ghana, hope it helps. I'm wearing a fluorescent yellow top, so I'll be easy to see!'

Even later ...

JONATHAN AGNEW: We've been asking people what they were doing when they heard Andrew Flintoff running out Ricky Ponting. Well, Felix in Sale has contacted us: 'I was dealing with water pouring through my ceiling from a burst pipe as Ponting was run out. I'd put a screw through my own pipe so Freddie cheered me right up.'

JD has also got in touch to say he was also suffering at the key moment. 'I was being dumped by my girlfriend at the exact moment Ponting was run out. At least I had Freddie's heroics to make me smile.'

And we've also heard from Brendan in Phoenix, Arizona, who told us he was listening via wireless speakers lying on a sunbed floating in a swimming pool – 'Unfortunately the excitement of the wicket led me to capsize and lose transmission.'

England v Australia, The Oval, August 2009

• • •

ED SMITH (*reading an email from Fred Boycott of Pudsey, a fictional Twitter account*): In Test matches Geoff Boycott has a better bowling average than Jonathan Agnew, a specialist bowler. Can you offer any explanation for this apparent anomaly?

GEOFF BOYCOTT: Yes, Fred. Geoffrey Boycott was a better bowler. He swung the ball ... Jonathan was just a seamer, straight up and down, with a little bit of movement off the seam. He never really swung the ball.

ES: Swing was the key ...

GB: Swing was the key. The other thing, Fred, he should've bowled with a cap on. That was his problem. He just bowled with that mop of hair all over the place. And let me tell you some other things: he keeps saying he bowled me out in first-class cricket, and I had it checked by our scorer. He got me out in the County Championship once, 26 June 1985 at Bradford, caught one. Butcher bowled Agnew four. And he got me out in that famous Benson and Hedges Cup match at Headingley, 5 May 1984, caught Hayman bowled Agnew six. And I got zillions of hundreds against Leicester when I were playing.

ES: And by then you were 45 years old.

GB: I was. If I'd have got him when I were younger I would've walloped him.

JONATHAN AGNEW: I dispute those figures. Let me go and check them.

GB: I'm off for my lunch now after that.

ES: Well, this edition of Ask Aggers is off to a cracking start.

New Zealand v England, March 2013

Champagne Moments

The Ashes debut of Australian leg-spinner Shane Warne.

JONATHAN AGNEW: And now at last, the moment we've been waiting for, Shane Warne coming on. Taking off his floppy hat to reveal a shock of blond hair. He has an earring in one ear as well … certainly a member of the new generation of international cricketers, with a modern-style haircut.

TREVOR BAILEY: He hasn't got a ponytail, though.

JA: He hasn't got a ponytail but he does have one of these new shaved jobs. Two or three razor round the back and rather more hair on top. Anyway, here he comes now, he's going to bowl from the far end, which is the end where Peter Such did such damage during Australia's innings. 6 for 67 he took. I just wonder, Trevor. There must be a little pressure on young Warne's shoulders because he must know that his team are expecting him to come on and take a few wickets here, or at least turn the ball.

TB: Well, if he doesn't turn the ball then England will have a very good time indeed …

JA: Just rehearsing one or two deliveries there to Brendon Julian at mid-on. There's a slip and a short extra cover, a ring of three on the off side, three on the leg and a deep backward square leg. And here he goes, Shane Warne, off only two or three paces, he bowls and Gatting is taken on the pad – he's bowled! Well, Gatting is still standing there – he can't believe it. But that must have turned a very long way. We haven't got a view of this but it took his off stump. Gatting can't believe it. That is Shane Warne's first delivery in a Test match in England, he's comprehensively bowled Mike Gatting … that must have turned an awful long way. Mike Gatting is still walking off, shaking his head, he just can't believe it at all. He's bowled for four and England are 80 for 2. Warne, as you'd expect, is being surrounded by Australia's fieldsmen. They're all clapping him on the back but we can see the replay now. It's tossed up and pitches round and about … outside the leg stump and it absolutely … [*laughs*] that turns feet.

TB: That was a jaffa!

JA: It's taken the top of off stump.

TB: That was an absolutely beautiful delivery.

JA: He's got a huge smile on his face and who can blame him? That ball pitched outside the leg stump, Gatting played it with a perfectly straight bat …

That's unplayable, and that I'm sure will send a shock wave right through the England dressing room.

TB: That was a glorious ball. To me, that was the champagne moment.

England v Australia, Old Trafford, June 1993

• • •

JONATHAN AGNEW: Umpire Mitchley has given him out lbw! Cork has taken a hat-trick in the first over of the day! He's mobbed by his team-mates and he's flung to the ground and Hooper departs now. What a start. There's a standing ovation from this near-full house for Dominic Cork, and that must surely put a seal on this match. Carl Hooper, leg before, first ball. Umpire Mitchley thought about it for a moment or two, but like Junior Murray he seemed to get right across in front of his stumps and there's an elated-looking Dominic Cork mopping his brow, a hug and a kiss from Angus Fraser, the big fast bowler, who came over and shook him by the hand. It's the end of Dominic Cork's first over and he is wandering around; he doesn't know where to go at the moment. He's absolutely on cloud nine.

England v West Indies, Old Trafford, July 1995

VIEWS
FROM THE
BOUNDARY

*For more than three decades the Saturday lunchtime
interview has yielded many great moments. Here's a
small selection, including some snippets from other
celebrity visits to the* TMS *box ...*

Ben Travers, Lord's, 1980

BEN TRAVERS (*on W. G. Grace, whom he met*): Like
another very large man, G. K. Chesterton, he had
a curiously falsetto voice, coming out of so huge a
frame. He was incidentally ... a practising doctor.
My mother was born and brought up in Clifton and
W. G. Grace was their family doctor. None of them
lived very long – except one, and she was a nun so he
couldn't get at her ...

BT: There are two kinds of batsmen, Brian, aren't
there? There is the batsman who says, 'I'm going to
slaughter you,' and the batsman who says, 'You can't
get me out.'

• • •

Michael Bentine, Lord's, 1983

I didn't even wear a box in those days – I wasn't all that well developed.

MICHAEL BENTINE (*recalling his days as a schoolboy cricketer*)

...

Richard Stilgoe and Peter Skellern,
The Oval, 1983

RICHARD STILGOE: It's very difficult, because like everybody else who can't play cricket, I bowl slow leg-breaks. Or I say they're slow leg-breaks and we just happen to be unlucky and they're not turning today. I am in fact the natural successor to Underwood, but no batsman in the world knows this – so they hit me out of the ground.

• • •

Rory Bremner, Edgbaston, 1985

Impressionist Rory Bremner performed an impersonation of TV commentator Richie Benaud. Unbeknown to him, Brian Johnston had arranged for Richie to visit the box …

RICHIE BENAUD: Where are the royalties, I want to know?

RORY BREMNER (*still in Richie's voice*): Oh, what a set-up …

• • •

Willy Rushton, The Oval, 1986

WILLY RUSHTON: [I've] never knowingly … made a nought, which is why I'm not wearing my Primary Club tie. I can't remember ever having made a duck, nor can I remember ever dropping a catch.

BRIAN JOHNSTON: They tell me your memory is not what it was …

• • •

John Cleese, Headingley, 1986

JOHN CLEESE: The great moments of sportsmanship do send a kind of thrill round the crowd, because they're a reminder that what's bringing us together is greater than the need to defeat each other.

• • •

David Essex, Lord's, 1989

BRIAN JOHNSTON: So you did some straight acting?

DAVID ESSEX: Yes, I played Byron at the Young Vic …

BJ: Did he win?

DE: No, he definitely lost.

• • •

John Major, Lord's, 1990

BRIAN JOHNSTON: I wonder when you have all these conferences, are you ever brought in notes with the final score?

JOHN MAJOR: Certainly, when I was Chief Secretary and we had great negotiations with colleagues over spending matters, the meetings did use to break up for critical parts of the Test match, to watch it.

• • •

Eric Idle, Lord's, 1990

BRIAN JOHNSTON: … [Eric Idle] lives within about a hundred yards of where I do and I've never seen him walking around St John's Wood …

ERIC IDLE: I have seen you …

BJ: Oh, you've never come up to me and asked for my autograph.

EI: I never came up to you because you were actually in the off-licence.

BJ: Oh …

EI: You were negotiating with the off-licence keeper, who was offering you some Christmas champagne, and you said, 'No, I don't need champagne because I'm given so much of it …'

BJ: Shhh! That's the voice of Eric Idle giving away a secret ... Do you mean to say you were in the shop then?

EI: I was in the shop. But I thought that was very impressive, that you don't have to buy Christmas champagne.

• • •

Peter O'Toole, The Oval, 1991

PETER O'TOOLE: I'm often asked why cricket means so much to me. And it's this high drama. Tufnell comes on – takes a wicket. Botham returns – takes a wicket. Viv Richards, the great king, delays his entrance. Delays and delays and delays. Finally he comes in with a couple of balls to play before lunch to a standing ovation. And of course he could have been out first ball.

• • •

Ian Richter, Old Trafford, 1992

Richter, a British businessman, had been imprisoned in Iraq for more than five years before his release in 1991. Brian Johnston asked him if he received the ball-by-ball commentary during his time in captivity in Baghdad.

IAN RICHTER: For the first three years I was in solitary, so I had virtually nothing. But eventually I got a radio and I started playing with it. And I managed to get a copy of *London Calling*, which announced they were having a ball-by-ball service and I tuned in quite fruitlessly one morning. I then, quite by chance, discovered that if I listened to a certain frequency, once it had finished shortly after UK lunchtime, if I twiddled the nob a little further to the left, I would pick up the South Eastern wavelength, where it was being beamed to. It was rather faint, but if I cocked an ear to one side and told everyone to shut up – I was rather fierce about that – I would have four or five hours' cricket. So it was wonderful.

• • •

Roy Hudd, The Oval, 1993

This was to be Brian Johnston's last 'View from the Boundary'. He died in January 1994.

BRIAN JOHNSTON: I'm told that at one time – before you were a Redcoat [*at Butlins*] – you were a sugar shoveller.

ROY HUDD: I'm glad you said that right, Brian.

BJ: I took care.

• • •

Archbishop Desmond Tutu, Lord's, 1994

The Archbishop dropped into the TMS *box during South Africa's first Test in England since the lifting of the international sporting ban.*

JONATHAN AGNEW: [Gough] bowls to Peter Kirsten and there's appeal for a catch. Kirsten is not moving but Dickie Bird is now seeing him on his way. The finger goes up.

DESMOND TUTU: Oh dear.

JA: And England have taken their fourth wicket, much to Archbishop Tutu's dismay.

DT: Oh, how horrible. We were coming to thump you here, man!

JA: Well, you may still do that …

• • •

Dennis Skinner, The Oval, 2000

HENRY BLOFELD: I was very nervous about interviewing you today, because you once said, 'I hate interviews. Elitist crap!'

DENNIS SKINNER:

Well, I don't regard you as elitist. You went to Eton, didn't you?

HB: Yes.

DS: I've been surrounded by people in this box – they're like me. They went to a run-of-the-mill school. And, anyway, some of these toffs like yourself can be pretty down-to-earth when it matters. How's that for a compliment?

HB: I take it as an enormous compliment …

• • •

Stephen Fry, The Oval, 2002

STEVEN FRY: I remember the days I used to go and watch Gower or someone warming up in the nets and you realize that even for him – an apparently sleepy, lyrical cricketer – it's such a hard game. It's a physical game. It's really tough and more so year after year. It's a hard, fast, sharp game, where balls grind into knuckles and you dive and graze your skin. It's not this fleecy, lovely thing that everyone thinks it is.

It's a wonderful game because it's evolved – like the language. It's not a museum piece and anyone who thinks cricket is, is daily missing out on the real joy of it.

• • •

Hugh Cornwell, Trent Bridge, 2005

Cornwell played the Stranglers' hit 'Golden Brown' on summarizer Mike Selvey's acoustic guitar.

JONATHAN AGNEW: Fabulous. And now Mike Selvey knows what his guitar should sound like. You see, if all punk music sounded like that I think I'd have liked it. But it rather passed me by …

• • •

Sir Elton John, Lord's, 2006

ELTON JOHN (*recalling the 2005 Ashes*): And I remember watching the one we won by two runs [at Edgbaston] and I couldn't bear it. I was in the South of France and I was on the phone to Michael Caine, saying, 'For God's sake.' And he was saying, 'I can't look!' Michael Caine is a huge cricket fan …

• • •

Daniel Radcliffe, Lord's, 2007

DANIEL RADCLIFFE: … So far I've got Andrew Strauss's photograph and Sachin Tendulkar's.

JONATHAN AGNEW: Were they aware who was asking for their autographs?

DR: No, they weren't. They were doing the thing that I do when I'm in a crowd of people, which is just keep your head down and keep moving as you sign. So I don't think any of them saw me.

JA: This is rather odd because I have behind me, I have to confess, a book from Andrew Strauss for you to sign for his child …

• • •

Radcliffe was to return to the box in 2009. Earlier that summer, he had texted TMS *to inform Aggers that he had discovered his scoring rate as a batsman in international one-day cricket was quicker than that of Geoffrey Boycott's (Aggers had only played one ODI, scoring two off three balls – Boycott had scored 1082 runs in 34 innings). He decided to lay a trap for the Yorkshireman …*

JONATHAN AGNEW: Welcome back, Geoffrey. You won't have heard my discussion with Victor just now but I presume you'd agree with me that a batsman with a strike rate of 66 must be a better player than one whose scoring rate is only 53?

GEOFF BOYCOTT: Well, that's right. Mind you, I'd have to see how many times they'd batted to be absolutely sure.

Aggers tried for some time to argue his case but Boycott would not be dissuaded. Eventually Aggers confided that the source of the information was the Harry Potter star.

GB:

I'll have that bloody little wizard!

A few weeks later, Boycott had his chance as Daniel Radcliffe appeared on TMS, *interviewed by Aggers.*

GB: Hey, and this little wizard, he's the one who texted you from New York about my battin'. Yeah, I've been looking for you. I'll get a bigger wizard and I'll change you into a mouse.

DANIEL RADCLIFFE: I'm only about double the size of a mouse.

GB: You're a little 'un, I'll tell you that.

JONATHAN AGNEW: Thank you, Geoffrey …

• • •

Russell Crowe, July 2009

The New Zealand actor, the cousin of former New Zealand batsmen Jeff and Martin Crowe, visited the TMS box.

JONATHAN AGNEW: We have a very welcome guest in our commentary box now. We have the cousin of the match referee.

RUSSELL CROWE: Good afternoon, Jonathan. Good afternoon, folks.

JA: Russell Crowe. Good to have you. Have you ever had that introduction before?

• • •

Lily Allen, The Oval, 2009

JONATHAN AGNEW: They're quite brave to take you on – boyfriends and things. Because that opens up their lives, too.

LILY ALLEN: Let's not go there, Aggers. Let's move on …

• • •

David Cameron, Lord's, 2013

Prime Minister David Cameron paid a visit to the TMS *box and admitted he was trying to avoid Geoff Boycott … he failed.*

DAVID CAMERON: [*sees Geoffrey Boycott*] Oh, here he is.

JONATHAN AGNEW: I've got some bad news for you …

GEOFF BOYCOTT: I've been inviting him to Headingley but he's too busy.

DC: I know. There's no Headingley Test in this series?

GB: One-dayer.

DC: Right.

GB: Don't get out of it.

DC: Right.

JA: If you've got nothing better to do …

DC: OK.

GB: That Question Time you do, say, 'Not today. I'm off to see Geoffrey Boycott at Headingley.'

DC: You think that would be a legitimate excuse?

GB: Yes. Ed supports me …

DC: Oh very good …

GB: … he has a constituency in Yorkshire.

DC: We'll have a day where we all cancel Question Time and we all come and watch the cricket.

The day after David Cameron visited the box, it was the Leader of the Opposition's turn …

JONATHAN AGNEW: Ed [Miliband], you were there when Geoffrey scored his 100th hundred.

ED MILIBAND: I was.

JA: You were. As a small boy.

EM: As a seven-year-old. I watched a replay of it recently, to do a message for your two-man show and it was exactly as I remember it. The thing I remember most of all was someone stealing your cap …

GEOFF BOYCOTT: A Lancastrian … He was a good one. He brought it back eventually.

Champagne Moments

With one ball to go in the day, Australian captain Steve Waugh, who had been under pressure after a poor run of batting form, was on 98, two short of a century in front of his home crowd.

JONATHAN AGNEW: Here we go, [Richard] Dawson comes up and bowls to Waugh, who drives ... and drives through the off side for his hundred! That is extraordinary! And Steve Waugh, a man of little emotion, can barely restrain himself now. His helmet's off ... he's waving his bat, Alec Stewart shakes his hand. You could not have scripted anything more remarkable than what we have seen here this afternoon.

Australia v England, Sydney, January 2003

• • •

JONATHAN AGNEW: In comes Harmison, he bowls a slower ball – he's bowled him! What an amazing delivery! That is absolutely stunning! Clarke has been bowled by a looping slower ball. He was softened up by three balls of searing pace, he fended two off his nose, and then in the most extraordinary bluff, Harrison bowled a ball, well, slower than Ashley Giles, I reckon. It completely deceived Clarke – it just about knocked the bails off. It was an extraordinary piece of bowling and that really does put the game back England's way again.

England v Australia, Edgbaston, August 2005

• • •

HENRY BLOFELD: Flintoff starts in, with this rather mincing tread of his, he's up to the wicket now, he bowls, Gilchrist edges and … it's an absolutely staggering catch by Strauss! He edged it and Strauss flung himself absolutely miles to his left and, one-handed, somehow managed to hold on. He held on as he rolled over – it was an extraordinary effort … My goodness me, Vic, what a catch.

VIC MARKS: He had to stretch away to his left, a fierce ball from Flintoff, off the back foot, outside edge, he starts to go with two hands, realizes he's not going to get there, sticks out his left hand – he is left-handed so I suppose that's a minor help – and, glory be, it stuck!

England v Australia, Trent Bridge, August 2005

FRANTIC
FINISHES

It is during a tight finish to a match that TMS *often comes into its own, as the nation stops and crowds around its radios.*

JOHN ARLOTT: That was the third ball. If it goes five balls there'll be no commentator left … He [Bedser] swiped at it and it hit him in the stomach. It was going a foot over and five thousand people appealed and I don't blame them …

[*England score one run*] They didn't dare try the overthrow. I don't think either of them had sufficient nerve or sufficient wind – and I certainly have no wind at all. Two balls, one wicket and two runs and the two wickets could come just as easily as the one run. It's a tie and two balls to go and Lindsay Tuckett's got to bowl. And he's bowling to Gladwin, and it's a bouncer, it's outside the leg stump and Wade, in an attitude of prayer, prevents it from being byes. And the next one they've got to run whatever happens. Tuckett to Cliff Gladwin, one run to win and one ball to go, and he's knuckled it, and they're running, and Bedser isn't run out and they've won off the last ball of the last over.

… And any sane man would tell you that England have won by two wickets. If you wanted to put it in a book, no one would ever believe it. It belongs to a novel, not *Wisden*. Never in all my life have I imagined I would see such a finish … For anyone with any patience, Gladwin made seven, and neither I, Gladwin, the bowler nor anyone else could tell you how he made them.

South Africa v England, Durban, December 1948

• • •

With seven runs required, two wickets left – one of them Colin Cowdrey, who had broken his forearm, and one over to bowl, the country was brought to a standstill.

ALAN GIBSON: Allen is three; seven runs are needed for an England victory, two wickets to fall, four balls left. And Hall bowling out of the background of the dark pavilion on a dark and gloomy evening, and after his little bit of excitement there when he

followed up and nearly fell over himself, he's looking
understandably very weary indeed as he trudges
back to his mark. A tremendous feat of fast bowling
this, by Hall, and if the West Indies don't win it
seems sad that such an almost superhuman effort
of valour should not have been in a winning cause.
Four balls to go, Hall comes in, bowling to Allen,
bowls to him and Allen plays that down to long
leg. There's one more run there ... 228 for 8. Allen
goes on to four, six runs are needed and three balls
are left as Shackleton has the bowling. A feverish
atmosphere now as Hall comes in with three balls to
go and bowls to Shackleton, and Shackleton flashes
outside the off stump, doesn't get a touch and they
go through for a very quick single and Shackleton's
going to be run out, he's run out! ... 228 for 9, they
[the teams] are not coming in, we must therefore
presume that with two balls to go Cowdrey will
come in. But Allen, as a result of the batsmen having
crossed, has at least got the bowling so Cowdrey may
not have to face a ball. And the applause seems to
indicate to me that Cowdrey is coming out and the
cheering tells you in fact that he is. There are two

balls to go, England needing 234 to win are 228 for 9, with Cowdrey, his left forearm in plaster, coming out to join Allen. Cowdrey is of course 19 already, having retired hurt, and the crowd now swarming out of the stands … the West Indians particularly, coming up eagerly right around the boundary rope waiting to charge on to the field as soon as this dramatic and gripping Test match has ended. And end it is bound to, either in the next ball or the one after that because there are only two left, six to win.

Here comes the first of them, Hall bowling to Allen, bowls to him and Allen plays it out on the off side and there is no run, and therefore with one ball left to go, barring any accidents like a no-ball, and I wouldn't put that beyond us – this game has had a surprise for us at every stage of its course. And Wesley Hall is going to bowl the last ball of the match from the Pavilion End to Allen. He comes and bowls it, and Allen plays defensively and the match is drawn, and the crowd comes swarming on the field. Cowdrey does not have to play a ball, the groundstaff, the policemen, are desperately rushing out to protect the sacred middle. The West Indies are being chased in by their own enthusiastic supporters. Wesley Hall, still with a tremendous run in him, leading the rush off the field. The end of a great game of cricket.

England v West Indies, Lord's, June 1963

• • •

The last stages of this match were played out at almost nine o'clock in the evening, in near total darkness. The scores were level after Lancashire's David Hughes had struck 24 off a John Mortimore over.

BRIAN JOHNSTON: Proctor coming in, I can just see him emerging from the gloom at the far end, bowling to Jackie Bond and he bowls this, he hits it up to mid-on … they won't run, though. Davey fields, and all the small boys are ready to run on. They've been running on with excitement, just now when that six was hit. They've stopped one or two fielders from stopping fours. Tremendous excitement … they're waiting around the ropes now … Lancashire needing one run to win [*crowd starts chanting*] and listen to this. Yes, this is a cricket match! It's cricket, you wouldn't think it in this light, you can hardly recognize them. Luckily they're wearing white flannels, one can see them in the dark. Two more balls this over and after that there will be three overs to go, so Lancashire only need one run, they have three wickets in hand and of course they will get it, they must … People waiting, the hands of the pavilion clock at five to nine, it's completely dark now, quite impossible for cricket really. Here's Proctor bowling to Bond and he hits this one, and it's gone through for one run on the off side! Lancashire are in the final! Lancashire have won …

Lancashire v Gloucestershire, Gillette Cup semi-final, July 1971

CHRISTOPHER MARTIN JENKINS: Here's Hendrick again, running in to bowl to Marsh, 63 not out, Marsh swings it high on the off side, Randall's underneath it, this could be the Ashes for England … He's caught it! They've won … Randall turns a cartwheel, the stumps are seized by the players, the crowd come on to the field, England have regained

the Ashes. A really wonderful moment for Mike Brearley, for Hendrick who took the wicket, for all the England side who have so outplayed Australia …

England v Australia, Headingley, August 1977

• • •

HENRY BLOFELD: Ian Botham is going to have one last crack at Jeff Thomson. 288 for 9, four to win for Australia, three to tie, Thomson has 21 and Border 62. And Botham now bowls to Thomson. Thomson plays. He drops it … and he's out! He's caught in the slips! Tavare knocked it up and it was Miller who caught the rebound. England have won by three runs and the England fielders are running off the ground, snatching the stumps. Poor Thomson and Border walk back utterly dejected. England have won by three runs, equalling the lowest margin of victory. What an astonishing end to the match.

Australia v England, Melbourne, December 1982

• • •

HENRY BLOFELD: So all of you listening around your radios, wherever in Australia you are, really can charge those glasses now. I give you my final, final permission. Ten are needed off one ball and even Professor Peter Roebuck [*summarizer*] is scratching his head trying to think how that could be done. All round the ground people standing up, yelling, just thrilled to be here, to have taken part, to have seen … bonfires are going in the stand at the far end, flares are being lit, my goodness me. Here comes McDermott, the last ball he bowls, Foster swings it away to backward point, they get two, that is the end, 246 for 8, Australia have won by seven runs. They jump into each other's arms, they whip up the bails, the stumps as souvenirs, they're all hugging each other and well they might. Australia have won the 1987 World Cup final …

England v Australia, World Cup final, Kolkata, November 1987

• • •

South Africa needed 22 from 13 deliveries when rain halted the match. Play restarted 12 minutes later but under the World Cup rules of that time South Africa's chase had been revised – they now needed 21 off only one delivery …

NEVILLE OLIVER: I notice the cluster of officials down in front of the members are in the same position. Now Alan Lamb believes that he knows the rules … and now we've got one ball to be bowled [*hollow laughter from co-commentator Peter Roebuck*] I can really tell you that as a lover of this game I almost feel disgusted to have to broadcast it. What an absolute joke. Oh, that is a disgrace. That is a disgrace. Well, that makes a farce of the World Cup. I really believe that. Look at the refuse coming out on to the ground. Here comes the last delivery. Lewis walks in at half rat-power and it's just pushed gently away towards midwicket, a run will be scored and the game's over [*boos from crowd*]. You couldn't imagine a worse ending than that. England have won the game by 20 runs and a contest that promised so much has finished up like a bomb that didn't go off …

England v South Africa, World Cup semi-final, Sydney, March 1992

• • •

England needed 13 off the last over to win and 11 off four balls. Then Nick Knight hit a six off Heath Streak …

HENRY BLOFELD: And he hit it like a kicking horse. That almost brought the balloon down, it went so high. Now we really are going to take our time. Andy Flower is coming out from behind the stumps to speak to Heath Streak. Nick Knight is standing there looking entirely unconcerned. Darren Gough is merely thinking, 'Thank goodness I'm not on strike at the moment.' David Lloyd [*England's then coach*] is down below us and looking as though he's got if not all the cares in the world on his shoulders, at least most of them. And what a moment for him …

Well, here he comes. It's Streak in to Knight and Knight can't reach that outside the off stump.

Has umpire Robinson called a wide? Peter Baxter
does in the box – but umpire Robinson certainly
doesn't and I think actually it was a bit exaggerated
because Knight did move away to leg.

Knight is standing there, Gough is giving him a
little bit of advice. Knight has got 92, the score is
200 for 5. Just five runs needed to win, two balls to
be bowled. And here comes Heath Streak again, he's
coming off his short run, he's bowling now. It's a full
toss. Nick Knight scythes it down the ground, Grant
Flower picks up, they're going to get two, he throws
in … No! It can't be run out because the bowler
Streak dropped the catch and took the bails off with
his hand. So two more runs. Three are now needed
off the last ball. Isn't it tremendous?

What's the betting someone is going to panic
under the pressure of it? Goodness me, one ball to
go, three runs to win, it's 202 for 5, Nick Knight
has got 94, Darren Gough has three and absolutely
everything is possible – not everything obviously,
obviously a Zimbabwe win isn't possible. What
excitement …

Anyway, it all comes down to this, the last ball of the match. Five days have gone into it. Many, many balls, much happening, and here comes the final ball. Three to win, Streak is in, he bowls to Knight, Knight makes room and slogs this into the off side. It's fielded there at deep cover by Grant Flower, they're coming back and there's going to be a run out! He is, he's run out! Gough has gone [*Knight was in fact run out*], the scores are level and the match is drawn. And Zimbabwe have got away with it.

Knight is despondent, he's very sad, you can see his shoulders down as he walks off. Gough is striding out. The Zimbabweans are thrilled, they're congratulating everyone. But what a game of cricket. Nick Knight steered England to the very brink of victory and couldn't quite get there. 204 for 5, the scores level, but this was a Test match and the game's drawn. So England by the narrowest of squeaks have failed to win this match. Now I think we should all go off to hospital to have our pulses checked.

England v Zimbabwe, Bulawayo, December 1996

• • •

A number of the TMS *commentators contacted during the research for this book cited this tense finale as one of their favourite pieces of* TMS *commentary. The game went down to the final over. South Africa needed nine off six balls with their last pair, Lance Klusener and Alan Donald, at the crease.*

TIM LAINE: … South Africa need nine runs to win it, and they can do it now. What pressure. What pressure on the batsmen. What enormous pressure on the bowler, who will be Damien Fleming. And what pressure on every fieldsman, not to mention all three umpires.

VIC MARKS:

It's a doddle in here, though, isn't it?

TL: Oh, it's easy.

VM: Well, it's Damien Fleming, who's got the privilege – or the nightmare – of bowling this last over. Somehow he's got to restrict Klusener to a single.

TL: Klusener 22 from 12 balls and at that rate he'll win the match for South Africa.

VM: Well, he seems to be impervious to pressure. He's got one way of playing and he sticks to it, come what may.

TL: Suddenly Australia, with its back to the wall. Nine to win, start of the fiftieth, Fleming in, bowls to Klusener, who swings along the ground for four! That went like a bullet through extra cover! And South Africa now just need five from five. Australia need a wicket … 209 for 9. Klusener 6, 1, 4 … 11 from three balls. We'd better get Gerald back [*de Kock, South African commentator*].

VM: That was a fantastic shot. He timed it brilliantly. It was full in length, it was almost where Fleming wanted it except there was width, just enough width, for Klusener to swing his arms. And he hit it like a tracer bullet about 10 or 15 yards to Tom Moody's left on the deep point boundary. He had no chance of stopping it.

TL: Paul Reiffel cuts a lonely figure out at third man on the rope. He had it between his hands and it slipped through [*Reiffel had dropped Klusener in the previous over*]. Five balls left, Fleming in and bowls, and Klusener thrashes at this, through long-off for four more! Scores are level! Unbelievable hitting by Klusener. And South Africa now, poised at the brink of an unforgettable victory ...

VM: ... He hit that first one hard – he hit that one even harder. No chance of long-off stopping that. This is half the problem – you aim for the yorker and if you don't quite get it up there it's right in the slot for Klusener and, my goodness me, he hit that hard, all along the ground. They can't watch in the South African dressing room ...

TL: 31 from 14 balls, the man of the World Cup, Lance Klusener, needs to score one more run to put his country into its first final. There are four balls left, a wicket in hand – and a wicket would put Australia in the final, a tie would have Australia in. South Africa need to win it. They're [*the Australian fielders*] all up now, they're all up. There's a couple of slips – they are all in the circle. Klusener adjusts his helmet. Fleming decides on a different line. He's going to come over the wicket to the left-hander instead and try and slant one across him …

Here it is, Fleming in and bowls and Klusener hoiks at it, doesn't score a run. There must be a run-out at the bowler's end! Lehman underarms and misses. Donald might have been out. The ball was dragged to mid-on by Klusener. Lehman got on to it, had a go, Donald was backing up …

VM: We're having a look at that replay. Lehman very close in at mid-on, shies at the stumps, underarm … he'd have been out if he'd hit.

TL: Well, another chance. Another one goes begging. Three balls left, one to win, Fleming in and bowls, Klusener hits back past the bowler, there's a mix-up! Oh, there could be a run-out! There will be a run-out! It's a tie! Australia is in the final! Australia is in an unprecedented fourth World Cup final! After an unbelievable tie at Edgbaston. Donald has been run out after an incredible mix-up. South Africa all out 213. The match is tied and Australia go to Lord's.

VM: Who writes your scripts, Tim? That is the most amazing finish to a one-day game I've ever seen. We had just come to terms with the fact that South Africa were going to win it from nowhere, when … that last ball wasn't hit powerfully, but it was hit to mid-off, Klusener came down the wicket, Donald halted, the fielder threw at the bowler's end where two South African batsmen were arriving, and then had the good sense to underarm to the keeper's end and, well, this is just incredible. The Aussies can't believe it, they are cock-a-hoop. The South Africans must think they are destined never to win the World Cup final. Klusener had just about got them there with phenomenal hitting but both Klusener and Donald ended up at the same end. Donald was about ten yards adrift minus his bat when absolutely astonished, stunned, and delirious Australians removed the bails. That was a fantastic game of cricket. What they must be feeling like in that South African dressing room I don't know.

TL: Really there was brain fade between the two batsmen, but that's what pressure does …

Australia v South Africa, World Cup semi-final, Edgbaston, June 1999

• • •

England had set New Zealand an improbable 550 to win in their final innings, but a blistering innings by Nathan Astle caused them a few palpitations ...

HENRY BLOFELD: Here comes Hoggard again, everyone is holding their breath. He's up to the wicket, he [Astle] is down the wicket, he swings, and he's caught behind! He's out! Foster claims the catch! England have won! Foster can hardly believe it! Nor can all the rest of the England side! And poor old Nathan Astle has gone for 222 ... Nelsons again! I knew Nelsons would get him somewhere! Double Nelsons for Astle, and New Zealand all out for 451. But what an incredible performance by Nathan Astle. For my money he can have man of the match, man of the series, man of the decade for that. It was a wonderful innings the like of which I don't think we'll ever see again. It was not slogging. Don't you think Nathan Astle just threw his head back ... he may have thrown caution to the winds but he played pure cricket strokes. It was a wonderful exhibition and for England the relief is unbelievable.

It was an innings which was a triumph for cricket and, however partisan you are, anyone who is on this ground today has to say they have seen something that in all probability they will never see again. Bill now wants to say something.

BILL FRINDALL: England have won by 98 runs.

HB:

My dear old thing, how kind of you to let us know.

New Zealand v England, Christchurch, March 2002

• • •

As Australia closed in on an improbable victory, Jim Maxwell and Geoff Lawson took over the microphone. It is TMS *custom to allow visiting commentators to call the final moments of their nation's victory. But there was to be another twist …*

JIM MAXWELL: It's down to three to win. The tie comes into the discussion now, I suppose, as a possibility.

GEOFF LAWSON: Two to tie, three to win. You don't want a couple of no-balls here.

JM: England striving for this last wicket. They've been doing that for a while. Harmison comes up and bowls, and Kasprowicz goes back and parries one – is he caught down the leg side!? I think so! There's an appeal for a catch and he's out!! England have won! England have won by two runs!

GL: Wow! What a finish! What an incredible Test match! That is astonishing stuff! Steve Harmison takes the final wicket and Geraint Jones takes a very good catch down the leg side. What a phenomenal Test match!

JM: Amazing finish. Billy Bowden waited for a moment, and the England players are surrounding themselves and slapping each other on the back. Flintoff came over and shook Brett Lee's hand. Both the Australian batsmen just stood there, dumbfounded for a moment or two, that the game could have ended like that. They got so close. It would have been a miraculous win, and at the death Harmison has produced a lifting ball down the leg side that brushed Kasprowicz's glove, Jones has taken the catch, England have levelled the series in the most dramatic fashion.

England v Australia, Edgbaston, August 2005

• • •

Another unforgettable finish from an unforgettable summer.

JONATHAN AGNEW: 127 for 7. If anyone can do it for Australia it's Shane Warne. But he won't be able to do it all in this over. England need two to win.

Warne comes in to bowl to Giles, who turns it away
through midwicket! That's it! England have won
the Test match! The batsmen complete their two,
they're raising their bats as they do. What a climactic
finish to another remarkable Test match, the third in
succession in this outstanding series. And who would
have thought it? That England, with one Test match
to play, now lead in this series by two matches to one.

England v Australia, Trent Bridge, August 2005

• • •

New technology such as Hot Spot can add to the drama
but also to the confusion in the commentary box ...

JONATHAN AGNEW: 296 for 9. Fifteen more to win.
Anderson runs in, bowls outside the off stump ...
he [Brad Haddin] drives and there's an appeal for a
catch behind! What's [umpire] Aleem Dar going to
do? Australia have no reviews. He's given it not out.
England *do* have a review available and they're
taking it!

PHIL TUFNELL: Hot Spot!

JA: That could be a Hot Spot. It could be the faintest Hot Spot …

PT: That is a Hot Spot …

JA: He's going to be caught behind.

GLEN MCGRATH: It [the Hot Spot] could have been there beforehand. The pad was in the way. You didn't see it there just a fraction …

PT: He's given it!

JA: England win the match by 14 runs! On the thinnest, faintest Hot Spot!

England v Australia, Trent Bridge, July 2013

Champagne Moments

ALISON MITCHELL: It's hugs and handshakes all round – and the tears are flowing for many of the side, who have worked so long and so hard to achieve this … We can hear now from Player of the Match, Nicky Shaw.

NICKY SHAW: I started the day crying, and I finished the day crying.

Later Alison spoke to England captain Charlotte Edwards …

CHARLOTTE EDWARDS: It's an amazing feeling to be world champions – it didn't matter how we got there as long as we got over the line. We told the girls they had to take their opportunities and Nicky has done that today with four wickets and seeing us home. I don't think it will sink in for a while, but this is a special moment and we'll remember this for the rest of our lives.

England v New Zealand, Women's World Cup final, Sydney, March 2009

• • •

CHRISTOPHER MARTIN JENKINS: Swann in again from the Vauxhall End. And that bites … he's caught at short leg! And it's Swann who's taken the final wicket, and Hussey, the hero of Australia, who's out. Hussey doesn't like the decision … but England now shaking hands with him. It was Cook who took the final catch. It's all over. England have regained the Ashes, after losing them so humiliatingly 5-0 in Australia only two years ago. Australia all out for 348 on a golden evening at The Oval.

England v Australia, The Oval, August 2009

• • •

England's Stuart Broad had just taken the wicket of M. S. Dhoni when Henry Blofeld came to the microphone.

HENRY BLOFELD: Well, it's Broad now who's going to bowl to Harbajhan Singh, the new batsman. Three slips, a gully, a backward point and a forward short leg. Here comes Broad, he's in, he bowls to Harbajhan ... oh, he must be out, he is! Lbw! He's gone first ball! It got him on the crease and he was absolutely plumb in front! And, goodness me, the celebrations are tremendous ... Broad's now on a hat-trick. Kumar has come in. We have four slips and two gullies and a forward short leg. Here's Broad – just listen to the noise – he's up to the wicket ... and he's bowled him! He's bowled him! He's taken a hat-trick! It's fantastic! Broad hit his off stump and Kumar is out. Three wickets in three balls, 273 for 8 and isn't it absolutely fantastic? It was an absolute humdinger of a ball – a beauty!

England v India, Trent Bridge, July 2011

CLOSE
OF PLAY

A. C. HUDSON (*Brian Johnston's housemaster*): You won't get anywhere in life if you talk too much.

• • •

Your voice is vulgar, but you have an interesting mind.

SEYMOUR DE LOTBINIERE (*BBC radio producer*) to John Arlott, 1947

• • •

This was John Arlott's final piece of TMS *commentary ...*

JOHN ARLOTT: Bright again going round the wicket to the right-handed Boycott, and Boycott pushes it away between silly point and slip, picked up by Mallett at short third man. That's the end of the over, 69 for 2, nine runs off the over, 28 Boycott, 15 Gower ... 69 for 2. And after Trevor Bailey it will be Christopher Martin Jenkins [*applause*].

TREVOR BAILEY: Well, the applause is ... I'm very lucky, really, to have been on while John completed his last commentary and on behalf of the *Test Match Special* team and listeners we thank him very much indeed. And will he open that bottle of champagne a bit quickish?

England v Australia, Lord's, September 1980

• • •

PETER BAXTER (*former* TMS *producer*): It's been suggested very often to me, usually by people trying to make changes to the programme, that our audience is very old … it is very interesting to see how much across the age range, and how far across the social range of the country, it does go. We have occasionally, from places like New Zealand in the middle of the night, wondered about and been fascinated to know who's listening. Because you do reach the point where you think there are two lorry drivers on the M6 who are the only people awake. And the raft of extraordinary things that come in from listeners … There's a vet fitting a pacemaker into a Scottie dog; there's a man who decided to save the maintenance of his lawn mowers until the middle of the night so he could listen to us while he worked on them … then there's this huge raft of students …

Date unknown

• • •

TMS *has jumped around the stations and schedules during its history, not always to everyone's approval …*

[*Orchestra finishes playing*] **ANNOUNCER**: You're tuned to Radio 3 FM and that was the last scheduled music on this frequency until, if all goes according to plan, about ten past six. Because in three minutes or so music gives way to cricket … Well, that's doubtless part of the National Arts Strategy, which we've been hearing about in *Third Ear* all this week. Don't blame the BBC, it was the Radio Authority, as was, who took away our medium-wave frequency … So you lucky cricket fans are spoilt for choice. Here on BBC3 FM, though, you do have the extra advantage of stereo cricket for the first time, which means that in a moment or two Jonathan Agnew will be where the first violins were. And Trevor Bailey will be approximately where the double basses were. Unless that is you favour the Stakhovsky or Kestrel layout with the basses in the middle … it's now known as the Brearley Position.

BBC Radio 3, 1992

• • •

JOHN ARLOTT (*in interview*): One doesn't invent things about cricket commentary because you don't need to invent them. There is so much happening all the time. You've got two things … three things. The actual mathematics of the game – they're essential, those you must keep up to date. Then you've got the mechanics of the play, which you're observing …

and you have the background of the play, the buildings outside, the people around the ground. And finally you have the history, of the whole game, not just this match. Sometimes the play itself is so dramatic that you have only time for the mathematics and the action … nothing of the surrounding circumstances and nothing of back history. But on other occasions when the play is quiet, surroundings and history … One tries to talk interestingly as if one was talking to a friend who couldn't see or who wasn't there and you were talking over the telephone to them.

Date unknown

SOURCES

The following books and audio sources were of invaluable help in compiling this book:

Books

Agnew, Jonathan, *Thanks, Johnners: An Affectionate Tribute to a Broadcasting Legend*, Blue Door, 2010

Baxter, Peter (ed.), *Test Match Special*, Queen Anne Press, 1981

—, *Test Match Special 2*, Unwin Paperbacks, 1985

—, *Test Match Special 3*, Queen Anne Press, 1985

—, *Test Match Special: 50 Not Out*, BBC Books, 2007

—, *The Best Views from the Boundary: Test Match Special's Greatest Interviews*, Icon, 2011

— and McNeil, Phil (eds), *From Arlott to Aggers: 40 Years of Test Match Special*, André Deutsch, 1997

— and Hayter, Peter, *The Ashes: Highlights since 1948*, BBC Books, 1989

— and Hayter, Peter, *England v West Indies: Highlights since 1948*, BBC Books, 1991

Johnston, Brian, *It's Been a Lot of Fun*, W. H. Allen,
    1984

—, *Rain Stops Play*, Unwin Paperbacks, 1985

Audio

John Arlott's Cricketing Wides, Byes and Slips!, BBC,
    2009

Johnners' Cricketing Gaffes, Giggles and Cakes, BBC
    Worldwide Ltd, 2008

'Voices of Summer', presented by Mark Pougatch,
    BBC Radio 5 Live, May/June 2013

'Test Match Special: Ball by Ball', presented by
    Rory Bremner, BBC Radio 4 – The Archive
    Hour, 2007

ACKNOWLEDGEMENTS

There are many people I need to thank, who willingly gave their time and memories. Adam Mountford, the current *TMS* producer, set me on my way. His predecessor, Peter Baxter, showed great kindness by not only sharing his memories, but also much of his archive. In no particular order, I'd also like to thank Jonathan Agnew, Henry Blofeld, Geoffrey Boycott, Harsha Bhogle, Simon Mann, Vic Marks, Mike Selvey, Jim Maxwell, Phil Tufnell, David Lloyd, Brian Waddle, Alison Mitchell and Neil Manthorp, who all happily gave their time to answer my questions and recall their favourite moments of commentary. Any errors are entirely of my own doing.

At BBC Radio 5 Live, Richard Maddock and Richard Burgess were of great help, particularly in putting me in touch with the BBC Archive. There, Kenneth O'Keefe went beyond the call of duty, answering my many queries and helping locate and dig out prized pieces of audio from the archive. Without his assistance, compiling this book would have been impossible.

At BBC Books, many thanks to Albert DePetrillo and Kate Fox for their patience and guidance. Finally, I'd also like to thank my agent Araminta Whitley and all the team at LAW.

INDEX